Cadette and Senior Girl Scout Interest Projects

Cadette and Senior Girl Scout Interest Projects

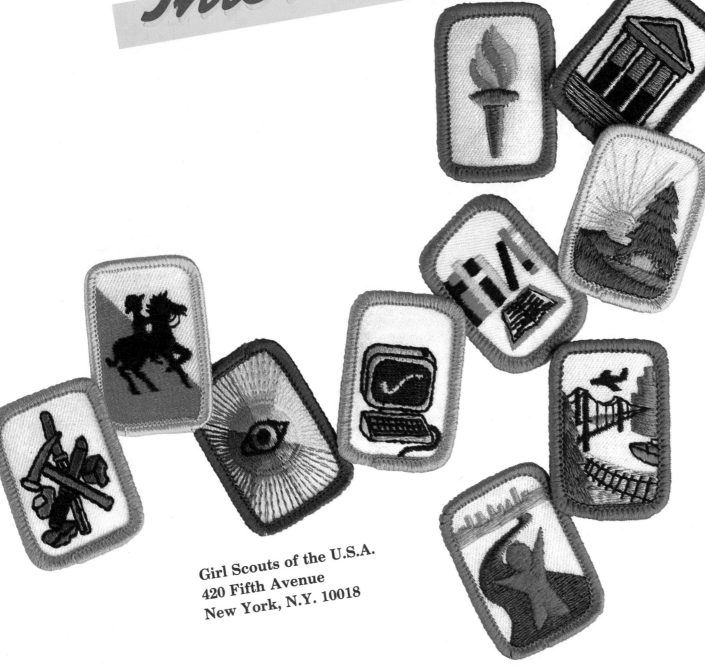

Girl Scouts of the U.S.A.
420 Fifth Avenue
New York, N.Y. 10018

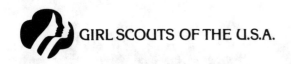
GIRL SCOUTS OF THE U.S.A.

Betty F. Pilsbury, President
Frances Hesselbein, National Executive Director

Inquiries related to the *Cadette and Senior Girl Scout Interest Projects* should be directed to Program, Girl Scouts of the U.S.A., 420 Fifth Avenue, New York, N.Y. 10018.

©1987 by Girl Scouts of the United States of America
All rights reserved
First Impression 1987
Printed in the United States of America
ISBN 0-88441-343-8

10 9 8

Director, Program Group
Sharon Woods Hussey

Project Director
Patricia Connally

Director, Graphics and Design
Michael Chanwick

Authors
Elisabeth K. Boas
Stephen Bohlin-Davis
Roberta Bourquin
Candace White Ciraco
Janie Cole
Patricia Connally
Gayle Ellis Davis
Bonnie Dawson
Sharon deNayer
Mary Gilmore Duhe
Toni Eubanks
Joan W. Fincutter
Cindy Ford
Carol N. Green
Mabel A. Hammersmith
Sharon Woods Hussey
Katherine Keena
Carolyn L. Kennedy
Donna L. Nye
Verna Lewis Simpkins
Lynn Ann London
Joan McEniry
Bonnie McEwan
Michele D. Montana
Harriet S. Mosatche
Elizabeth Munz
Corinne M. Murphy
Lynn M. Obee
Fran Powell
Nancy Hughes Richardson
Dehra W. Shafer
Roxanne Spillett
Valerie M. Tennent

Editor
David Sahatdjian

Design Studio
Keithley and Associates

Cover Design
Keithley and Associates

Contents

What Cadette and Senior Girl Scout Interest Projects Are All About

This book of interest projects is a collection of activities for you to do by yourself, with a friend, or in a group. Whether you have been a Girl Scout for many years, for one year, or are just starting, you can still enjoy doing one, several, or all of these activities. For the best results, you will find that using this book with the *Cadette and Senior Girl Scout Handbook* will enable you to see all the possibilities and potentials in your efforts.

Learning by doing — and having fun along the way — is what these interest projects are all about. You'll discover you can really make things happen with your friends and with the help of adults who have special knowledge and skills to share with you. Your adult partner — your leader, consultant, adviser, etc. — can support and guide you in choosing activities and projects that match your talents and fit your pace for doing and learning.

From Here to There

You'll find that each interest project has an introduction that describes the interest area and specifies the number of activities you must complete in order to earn a recognition. Some activities may be too difficult; others may be too easy. You can choose the ones that offer just the right amount of challenge for your personal growth. Because each person grows and learns at her own pace, you may take anywhere from a few months to a year to complete a project, depending upon the time you spend on each activity and the availability of resources.

What if none of these interest projects appeal to you right now? Then you can write your own by following the general format of the others (see page 7).

When you complete one or more of the interest projects, what next? Here are a few ideas for you to consider:

- Become a consultant in an interest project you have already tried.

- Work with your Girl Scout council or neighborhood association to tell other girls about interest project experiences available to members of Girl Scouts.

- Do a service project that depends on the knowledge and skills you've gained from an interest project.

- Work with your Girl Scout council to plan and carry out events that will help others with their interest project activities.

- Get a job related to your interest project experience.

- Apply your efforts to the Girl Scout Silver or Girl Scout Gold Award.

Now....
Are you ready for an adventure of your own choosing?

Planning, with your adult partner, will aid in choosing the best activities for you, in considering proper safety measures, and in utilizing local resources (people, places, and things). A lot depends on you and the decisions you make for yourself.

Finding an Interest Project

What would you like to do? Would you like to try Water Sports, or learn more about that game all your friends are playing by doing the Sports interest project? Do Wildlife or Camping attract you? Are you enthusiastic about Audiovisual Production or Fashion/Fitness/Makeup? Or are you more inclined to Visual Arts, Music, Photography, or Folk Arts?

If you're mulling over several projects, count the activities in each that really excite you. Remember to think about your own needs and the resources available to you in your community. Choose the project that has the most things you want to do, and save the others for later on. You could also decide to do some activities in an interest project as part of your other Girl Scout program activities.

Starting Out

Individually, or with a friend or your troop or group, draw up a tentative plan for carrying out your interest project activities. Include your leader and a consultant, if you've chosen one already, in your decision making.

These are some decisions you'll need to make:

* what activities you would like to do, or which alternate within an activity

* what you can expect of yourself — your goals, commitment, energy

* how much time you want to spend on each activity and on the interest project as a whole

* what you will do alone and what you will do with others

* how you will adapt activities to fit your local resources

* what consultant(s) you will need to help you (see pages 5–6 for more help in identifying, selecting, and approaching people)

* what other resources might be helpful, and where you can find them

* how you will get these resources — what can you borrow, share, or trade with another group; what resources you might request from community people, businesses, family, etc.; what printed materials are available in your local or school library

* how you can earn money for the activities (see page 8 for money-earning how-to's)

* how you will know when you have finished an activity

* how you will record your interest project plan

* how you will measure your progress (learning and skills development) as you go along and at the end of your interest project.

Linking Interest Projects to Other Girl Scout Program Activities

Cadette and Senior Girl Scouts have a great range of things to keep them busy. All members can go camping, participate in councilwide events, and see other parts of the country by traveling to any of the three Girl Scout national centers. If you are 14 years or older, you may embark on international travel by visiting one of the world centers. The *Cadette and Senior Girl Scout Handbook* has more information for you to read about all these possibilities.

If you find yourself planning to participate in a wider opportunity (see *Wider Ops*, a catalog mailed annually to all Cadette and Senior Girl Scouts) or preparing to travel to a Girl Scout national center or a world center, don't forget to look at the interest projects Travel, Money Management, Global Understanding, and any others relating to the event you'll be attending. Interest projects can help your planning and increase your fun.

Getting School Credit

Some schools have policies that allow students to design course work themselves or to get school credit for activities accomplished outside of regular classes. If your school has such a policy, you may be able to obtain school credit for doing your interest project activities.

First, contact your Girl Scout council to see whether the council has been working with your school or school district to arrange for credit. If not, explore the possibilities on your own.

If your school agrees to consider giving credit for interest project activities, you may need to work with a school representative (perhaps a teacher, guidance counselor, grade adviser, or principal) before beginning your project.

What you plan to do, whether or not a school staff member will supervise what you do, and how you will keep a record of what you do may determine how you proceed. Some schools may request that you do something beyond the activities suggested in an interest project — perhaps a final report or evaluation.

If your school is not ready to consider giving credit for interest project activities at this time, don't be discouraged. Maybe, as you and other girls from your school get involved in interest projects, your school representatives will recognize that a well-done project is an exciting learning experience equivalent to and deserving of school credit.

Finding Resources for Interest Projects

In Girl Scouting and throughout your community, you'll find all kinds of help to do your interest projects. People are often your best resource. When you think of getting someone to help you, don't just look for experts. Many other people can be helpful in interest project work. Ask other Girl Scout members and their friends if they know someone who may have the knowledge, materials, resources, etc., you need to do an interest project. Parents and other family members of Girl Scouts can provide numerous resources. You and other girls interested in working on interest projects can arrange a party or meeting with family members to share your goals with them and ask for their help.

Neighbors may be good interest project resources. Senior citizens have much knowledge, skill, and experience to share. Young professional people are often eager to share their special interest with Girl Scouts. Look for hobbyists, as well as people with unusual occupations.

Business and professional people are there for the asking. Guidance counselors and employment counselors from agencies or businesses can give you insights into the process of career decision making and job searching. Invite them to speak to your group.

Government resources — people as well as printed materials — are available. Government publications are often very helpful. Many resources are free or inexpensive. They cover a broad range of topics. Federal, state, and local government agencies have many helpful materials. Look in your local phone book and go to your library to find out more about these agencies. Consult the resource list on page 6 of this book.

You can attend workshops, seminars, or courses. Careers are a big part of people's thinking today, and workshops on career and life decision making are popping up all over. Why not take one? Many are free or inexpensively offered through religious organizations, schools, and women's and youth groups. They may provide you with the information or resources you need to use in an interest project.

Local libraries are an invaluable resource. You can explore using your school library as well as public, private, or other libraries in your area. Librarians are often very eager and willing to help people interested in learning new things.

Consultants

Once you have explored possible resources, you may decide you will need a consultant to help you with a specific interest project.

The person you're asking to help with your project will likely have a few questions before she or he makes any commitment.

For instance, why do you need help? You should be able to describe your interest project and how the activities you plan to do with a consultant fit into your other activities. Be ready to explain whatever experiences you may already have in your interest area and any expertise you have acquired. You may even need a consultant's help to find your own level of expertise. You'll want to be clear about what you want to accomplish and how much effort you intend to put forth.

Estimate how much time you are asking your consultant to give and how often you may need to meet with one another.

Describe the resources (materials, equipment, facilities) you have available or have arranged to use. For instance, you would want to tell the consultant that you have a first-aid book, that you can borrow a camera, or that the Girl Scout camp could be the site for a trail project or survival training.

Be prepared to discuss your own or your group's abilities and potential, as well as any limitations.

Also, consider whether distances, costs, or the setting will have any influence on the way the consultant works with you. If so, think about how you can help the project group cope.

4

Above all, explain to the consultant why you have chosen this interest project and the particular activities you have decided to do. Are you in it for fun? skills? career possibilities? preparation? new friends? community service? self-improvement? Your enthusiasm should be catching — so that the consultant can anticipate the satisfaction of her or his working with you, the rewards of helping someone grow, the opportunity to be involved in the community, the experience of a partnership with you, and the promise of your appreciation.

Making Connections

If you don't know the person, how do you make the first contact? What do you say?

Writing a letter is one way; telephoning is another. In either case, you will have to plan ahead.

This sample letter may give you some ideas on what to include in your letter. Be as specific as you can. Allow time for the consultant to read your letter and decide if and when she or he can help you.

```
                                        Date
                                        Street Address
                                        City or Town, State, Zip Code


     Consultant's Name
     Consultant's Title (if any)
     Organization
     Street Address
     City or Town, State, Zip Code


     Dear Ms. or Mr. (name of consultant):

     Because you have been identified as someone with a

     special knowledge of (name of activity), I hope

     you'll be able to help me work on a Girl Scout

     interest project called (name of project).  I need

     a consultant who will help me plan my efforts and

     give guidance on how to complete the activities.


     Would it be possible for you to meet with me?

     I would like to explain more about the interest

     project.  I am looking forward to your reply.

     Thank you for your consideration.


                              Sincerely,



                              (Your Name)
```

(Add telephone number and times to call.)

If you decide to telephone, rehearse a bit before you dial. Review the tips in "Consultants" and, if necessary, write down some of the answers before you call.

Whichever approach you choose, make certain that the person understands exactly what you expect. Be as flexible as you can, so arrangements for meetings and conversations can be convenient for the consultant. Whether or not the answer is yes, be appreciative of whatever time the consultant gives you. It would be nice to send a note of thanks to the person after your call. Who knows? You may have found a consultant for now or for later on.

Other Resources

You may find this list of organizations and associations helpful as you look for resources to do your interest projects. Be sure to research your local resources as well.

American Alliance for Health, Physical Education,
Recreation, and Dance
1900 Association Drive
Reston, Va. 22091

American Association for Counseling and
Development
5999 Stevenson Avenue
Alexandria, Va. 22304

American Association of Retired Persons
1909 K Street, N.W.
Washington, D.C. 20049

American Automobile Association
8111 Gatehouse Road
Falls Church, Va. 22047

American Camping Association
5000 State Road, 67N
Martinsville, Ind. 46151

AFS Intercultural Programs
313 East 43rd Street
New York, N.Y. 10017

American Folklore Society
Ohio Arts Council
727 East Main Street
Columbus, Ohio 43205

American Red Cross
17th and D Streets, N.W.
Washington, D.C. 20006-5099

American Youth Hostels
P.O. Box 37613
Washington, D.C. 20013

Association for Childhood Education International
11141 Georgia Avenue, Suite 200
Wheaton, Md. 20902

The Experiment in International Living
U.S. Headquarters, Kipling Road
Brattleboro, Vt. 05301

Future Homemakers of America
1910 Association Drive
Reston, Va. 22091

National Art Education Association
1916 Association Drive
Reston, Va. 22091

National Association for Search and Rescue
P.O. Box 3709
Fairfax, Va. 22038

National Association for the Education of
Young Children
1834 Connecticut Avenue, N.W.
Washington, D.C. 20009

National Association of Underwater Instructors
P.O. Box 14650
Montclair, Calif. 91763

National Audubon Society
950 Third Avenue
New York, N.Y. 10022

National Safety Council
444 North Michigan Avenue
Chicago, Ill. 60611

National Ski Patrol System
Ski Patrol Building, Suite 100
133 South Van Gordon Street
Lakewood, Colo. 80228

National Trust for Historic Preservation
1785 Massachusetts Avenue, N.W.
Washington, D.C. 20036

National Wildlife Federation
1400 16th Street, N.W.
Washington, D.C. 20036

Sierra Club
730 Polk Street
San Francisco, Calif. 94109

U.S. Committee for the
United Nations Children's Fund
331 East 38th Street
New York, N.Y. 10016

Women in Communications, Inc.
2101 Wilson Boulevard, Suite 417
Arlington, Va. 22201

Women's Sports Foundation
342 Madison Avenue
Suite 728
New York, N.Y. 10017

Writing Your Own Interest Project

Just now, your time and imagination may be taken up with something you really like to do that seems unrelated to any of the interest projects in this book. If you would prefer to continue your involvement with this specialized interest, you could write your own project. Here are guidelines to help you:

1. Follow the format established in this book.

2. Decide whether you will write the interest project alone or work in a group.

3. Make sure you include your leader and perhaps an interest project consultant, too. They will help you plan and should be aware of safety standards.

4. Write at least eight activities that you would like to do. Consider activities that will help you to do the following: develop skills you already have; teach new skills; increase your knowledge; discover career possibilities; give service; pursue a hobby; relate to people of both sexes, and to people from different generations, races, religions, ethnic groups, and cultures; measure your progress and set new goals.

As you write an activity, think about varying what you will be doing. For example, you wouldn't want eight activities requiring a trip or an interview. Make sure your activities are appropriate for your knowledge and skill levels. If they're too easy, you'll get bored; if they're too hard, you'll give up in the middle.

Know your resources, those within your community and those outside your community. Do some research to ensure that a resource or a consultant will be available.

When you have written your interest project, share it with these people:

* your possible consultants — for suggestions on improving it

* your Girl Scout council — so the council will know what you are doing and can help you by finding consultants and by planning council events to help you do the activities you have identified

* your Girl Scout troop or group, your friends and schoolmates — to let them know what you are doing and to see if they would like to join your interest project group as new or continuing members of Girl Scouting

* your family — so they will know what you are doing, what you are interested in, and how they can help you.

Earning Money for Interest Projects

By this time, you've probably read some of the interest project activities and have discovered that lots of them are free. But others sound as though they might be expensive. What if you select a project that seems costly? Should you change your plans? Not at all. If you think an activity is important and worth doing, it's worth the effort to find the necessary resources (things and money).

As an individual, you may be able to meet your needs by borrowing equipment, trading and exchanging resource materials, or making do with what you already have. If yours is a troop or group project, you should consider paying for it from money in your troop or group treasury or earning the money that is needed through an activity related to the project.

As you budget, you'll find yourself doing some activities from the Money Management interest project. Some of the activities in this project involve keeping records and deciding how to spend your money.

Important: Read Carefully

Before you undertake any troop money-earning project, your leader should obtain permission from your Girl Scout council for your troop or group to conduct the project. Also, ask your leader for a copy of *Safety-Wise* and study the program standards for money-earning projects.

Notice especially that "'troop money earning' refers to activities planned and carried out by girls and adults, in partnership, to earn money for the troop treasury." (*Safety-Wise*) It is very different from fund raising, which refers to any of various methods of soliciting contributed funds to support the Girl Scout council, and which is the responsibility of adults. Basically, that means you must not ask for cash donations toward project activities.

Next Steps to Take

Successful troop money-earning projects involve several steps:

1. Follow the standards in *Safety-Wise* and the laws and regulations of your council and community. For example, some health regulations limit bake sales.
2. Choose a product or service that you and your group can do well.
3. Sell a product or service that your customers and community need.
4. Get approval and advice from adults (parents, council people, etc.).
5. Work with your council to promote your project through lots of publicity that's early, consistent, and appealing.
6. Adjust your plans as you discover ways to improve your sales so that you will be likely to earn the money you need.

Think of ways to make money earning profitable in terms of experience as well as dollars. With skill and imagination, your troop or group could sell products or services and still be working on an interest project. Here are a few ideas to start you thinking.

Product/Service	Interest Project
food	Creative Cooking
screened T-shirts	Visual Arts
plants from seedlings	Plant Culture
recycling	Eco-Action
tournament	Sports, Water Sports
skills-building clinic	Sports, Outdoor Survival
carnival, play, or mime show	Energy Awareness, Community Time Capsule
party pictures	Photography
fashion show or beauty clinic, manicuring, haircutting	Fashion/Fitness/Makeup
car wash, safety inspection	Auto Maintenance

In planning any money-earning project, paying attention to all the details is like counting every penny. With pluck and luck, your ideas will add up to success!

Interest Projects

The World of Well-Being

Dabbler

What do I plan to do with my life? How do I get where I want to go? What do I value most in life? What decisions do I have to make? Perhaps these are questions you have asked yourself or will ask in the near future. Exploring the World of Well-Being will help you discover answers to these questions, plus more.

Knowing yourself, your strengths, weaknesses, interests, values, needs, and emotions are all part of planning a positive path to get where you want to go and getting to know the most important person in your life — you. Knowing how to take care of your body, make decisions, solve problems, cope with feelings, relate to others, and develop a knowledge of health and safety are essential ingredients of your total makeup. Knowing yourself doesn't stop with an interest project; it is a lifelong process.

The World of Well-Being deals with the way you think, feel, and act. The knowledge you gain from looking closely at yourself, combined with the experiences you gain, will give you the power to plan positive experiences and to set and achieve realistic goals for yourself. Remember, a safe, healthy, and happy future lies within you.

Complete eight activities.

1. Plan and conduct a beauty workshop. Invite consultants to talk with you about, or demonstrate solutions to, some of your concerns, such as skin, hair, makeup, teeth, dieting, and shaping up. Consultants might include a cosmetologist, dermatologist, beautician, dentist, physician, physical education teacher.

2. Create and present an action game or visual presentation (puppet show, skit, display) to help younger children understand the importance of good nutrition. You might include proper eating habits, basic food groups, required nutrients, snack foods, and body weight.

3. Keep a record of all the feelings you experience in one week. Write down whether each feeling is positive,

negative, or neutral. Have other members of your group do the same thing. Compare your feelings (and their origins) with those of the other people. Identify the five most common positive feelings and the five most common negative feelings. Discuss ways to manage your negative feelings. Analyze what situations contributed to your positive feelings.

4. Did you know that auto accidents are the leading cause of death between ages 15 and 24? Survey at least five friends to find out if they, or someone close to them, have been in an auto accident in the past year. Identify where and why the accident occurred. Design a presentation that can help others learn about this serious problem and the safety measures that can be taken to prevent automobile accidents and lessen injury and damage.

5. Plan an event such as a workshop, clinic, or demonstration to help you, your friends, parents, and others find answers to the many concerns teenagers have about adolescence. For example, relationships with boys; relationships with adults; the effects of smoking, drinking, and taking drugs; emotional and body changes. Ask parents, clergy, teachers, physicians, and other adults to assist you in planning this event. Books, magazines, and local or national organizations may also be helpful, reliable resources. Evaluate your plan along the way and at the end of the event.

6. Prepare a well-balanced international meal at home or on the trail for family or friends. Decide what you will serve and the type of entertainment to accompany the meal. Make arrangements for buying the ingredients, preparing the food, serving, and cleaning up. Add the recipes to your recipe file.

7. Volunteer to assist in a nursery school, day-care center, day camp, playground, or health or community center for at least 10 hours. First, observe the children, teens, or adults you will be working with. Then, help plan fun activities that are suitable for them.

8. Demonstrate your ability to perform first-aid skills by doing one or more of the following:

   • Assist a first aider for at least three troop meetings, a camp weekend trip, a blood donor drive, or at least two school or community sporting events.

   OR

   • Prepare and teach at least two lessons on first-aid skills, such as how to treat bleeding, burns, choking, poisoning, or how to give mouth-to-mouth resuscitation, at a school, religious, or community group meeting.

   OR

   • Create a play, slide show, or charts that provide helpful first-aid information to a school, religious, or community group.

9. Participate in one of the following events: a mini- or Special Olympics, bike-a-thon, walkathon, tournament, sports day, or New Games festival. Be sure you are physically prepared to participate in the event you select. A medical history and health examination are required for contact sports, and a medical history for noncontact sports. See *Safety-Wise*.

   OR

   Find out how one of these events is organized and, with the help of your troop, plan to hold one. Recruit all the necessary people, such as players, coaches, officials, scorers, timers, equipment managers. Select a safe place to carry out the event. Evaluate your plan along the way and at the end of the event.

10. Jot down at least five things you and your friends like to spend money on. Go comparison shopping and compare the cost, quality, care, and/or safety of these items. Then, design a booklet that gives teens tips on how to get the best buys for their money. You might include what to consider when purchasing these items, where and when to shop, fads, and advertising. Share this booklet with others.

11. With a group of family members or friends, brainstorm the various problems that occur within families, such as the effects of a natural disaster, a death, frequent fighting, a runaway, drinking, or drug problems. Discuss or role-play the different ways families can handle such problems to prevent being overwhelmed by them.

12. Keep an accurate record of all the things you do and the time you spend doing them for four to seven days. Include activities such as attending school, doing homework, watching television, reading, helping at home, working, traveling, dressing, eating, sleeping, visiting friends or relatives. At the end of the days, calculate the number of hours you spent on each activity. Make an advance weekly schedule that includes a hobby or leisure-time activity you have been wanting to do, but couldn't seem to find the time for. Decide how much time you will spend doing it. Try out your schedule. Revise it until it fits you.

Child Care

Do you take care of your younger brothers and sisters? earn money as a baby-sitter? want to prepare for a career working with children? think that being a parent may be part of your future? In this project you will find suggestions for taking care of children, enjoying sharing with them, and helping them grow.

Complete eight activities.

1. Arrange to observe a baby under the age of two. Look and see what you can learn by just watching or playing with this baby. What can this baby do by herself or himself? What does the baby like to do? Can the baby talk? walk? How does the baby communicate? What kinds of help does this baby need from other people throughout the day? Observe this baby several times and keep an observation notebook to record your findings.

   Now observe a young child between the ages of two and four. How does this child compare with the baby you have been observing? Can they do the same things? What are the differences? Do they need the same things? Record your observations in your notebook. How have your observations helped you understand children you know or take care of? If you enjoy this activity, you may want to observe other children or watch several children of different ages to see how they change as they grow.

2. What were you like when you were a baby? when you were two, three, or four years old? when you started school? What do you remember about yourself? Talk to people who knew you at different ages. Do they have pictures of you, stories about you, information about your health, where you lived, or who took care of you? Ask yourself, "What is special about me? What are those things in my life that make me the special person I am today?" Record what you find in a story about yourself, a poem, a song, a tape recording, or a diary, for

example. Maybe you will want to write a play about your life or paint a picture. Share some of these findings with your friends and family. Discuss ways you are alike and ways you are different.

3. Children like to play. When children play, they are learning about the world, about themselves, and about other people. What do the children you know like to do? Keep an idea file of games, songs, finger plays, and stories that children like. Include such things as recipes for play dough and finger paints. Talk to parents, nursery or day-care workers, or librarians for suggestions. Keep adding to your collection for use when you take care of your own younger brothers or sisters, baby-sit, or do volunteer work with children. You may want to volunteer to use your ideas in an early childhood center or at a library.

4. Do some research on toy safety. Find out what safety features to look for in a toy. Talk with salespeople, parents, lawyers, and people who work with children. Design and make a safe toy for a young child you know. Discuss the safety features of this toy with an adult before you finish it. When you are sure it is safe, introduce your toy to the child in a play situation. Does the child enjoy playing with it?

   OR

   Find out safety requirements for places where children spend time. For example, learn about the fire and health codes for day-care centers in your community. Check your own home for safety features. Make a list of ways you can help keep your home safe for children and adults. Share this information with your family.

5. Where can children in your community play and have fun? Locate the playgrounds and other recreational facilities in your area. Find out what ages can use them. Are they safe? What equipment do they provide? Are they supervised? Do they cost money? Can they be used all year or just during one season? Ask similar questions of your own.

Share your findings with friends and parents in your community. If you have a special interest in this topic, you may want to make a recreation guidebook, plan a recreation event for children in your community, or work with your community leaders to improve nearby play areas.

6. A growing baby needs to eat a balanced diet to stay healthy. Invite a child-care expert to talk about foods children need for healthy growth. Find out what babies eat at different stages of their development. What foods do infants, toddlers, and preschoolers need and enjoy? Use this information to help prepare a meal or a snack for a baby or young child. Notice children's reactions to different foods and how they act with the person who feeds or eats with them.

7. A baby's health begins before birth. Invite a health-care professional to talk to you or your group about how a woman's health contributes to the birth of a healthy baby. Include some of the following topics in your discussions: good diet, smoking, drugs, alcohol, proper rest, prenatal medical care, and inherited health factors. Assess your own personal health in light of what you learn.

8. Today, many mothers of young children work outside the home. Interview a mother who works outside the home full-time, one who works outside the home part-time, and one who does not work outside the home at all. Find out their child-care arrangements. What are the roles played in child rearing by fathers, grandparents, other family members, and professional child-care workers? What did the mothers tell you about the advantages and disadvantages of each arrangement? Compare your findings to what you think is an ideal situation.

9. Make a booklet or chart showing signs and symptoms of childhood illnesses. Make use of it at home or when baby-sitting. Include what to do for these illnesses or in emergencies for such things as burns, cuts, poisoning, choking, seizures, high fevers, or possible broken bones. Also, find out what immunizations children should have and when and why these are given. Make a permanent record of immunizations or special health needs for each member of your family.

OR

Work as a volunteer at a children's health facility. You might agree to read to a child, put on a performance, or be an aide for a specified period of time.

10. Role-play problem situations involving young children. For example, you might pretend to be a parent. How would you react to a child who has just broken something, taken something from another child, or hurt another child or a pet? How would you try to decide fairly when two sisters or brothers want to choose a different television program or bedtime story? Ask parents and others who care for children to help you identify effective ways to interact with a child or children in such situations. Share your ideas with your group members. Also, look for more than one way to respond to children's needs.

11. A child's life is not always fun and play. Some things that happen in life are troubling and hard to understand. These events may affect children in many different ways. Sometimes you can help children understand their world through a story or a play. Find or create a story, a puppet show, or a flannelgraph scene for young children of preschool or kindergarten age that presents one of the following situations in a sensitive and supportive way:

   * the birth (or adoption) of another child

   * being with children of different cultural, ethnic, or religious groups

   * the divorce of a child's parents

   * a family that is moving

   * a parent being out of work

   * going to the hospital for an operation.

Get ideas by role-playing the part of adults and children in these situations.

Because children of different ages look at the world in different ways and because you are dealing with important, sensitive issues, check with a professional for advice along the way. Be sure to have your finished product reviewed by a parent, librarian, preschool educator, health-care counselor, nurse, social worker, or child psychologist. Present your creative efforts to children in a library, nursery, preschool program, or health clinic waiting room.

12. Plan and conduct a workshop on a topic such as "Baby-Sitting Do's and Don't's," "Family Crisis: How Our Community Can Help," "What Parents Need to Know," "Careers in Child-Care Professions," or "Kids' Games." Ask professionals, parents, or children themselves for advice on planning and for assistance in the workshop itself.

Collecting

Collecting can be a lifelong hobby that provides you with the opportunity to learn and to increase the value of your collection. Developing a collection over a course of years ensures that you become proficient in the subject. It also offers you opportunities to interact with others who share your interest. And who knows — one day your collection may end up as a museum exhibit!

Complete six activities, including the two that are starred.

*1. Keep a written log on each item in your collection. Create a form for this purpose and number each item to correspond with its log number. Your form should include the following information:

- description of item
- date acquired
- location found or purchased
- cost (if applicable)
- personal appraisal.

Add at least a couple of new items to your collection during the year.

2. Plan a storage/display unit for your collection. You may build or create this unit. Arrange your collection for display or for easy access. Suggested units are plastic boxes, a simple wooden cabinet with drawers, or even a desk top or bookshelf.

3. Read magazines and books that will help you become a knowledgeable collector. Join or form a club for collectors in your community. Learn about their collections and exchange ideas and information with them. If possible, attend a convention or exposition on your type of collection.

*4. Give a 5- to 10-minute talk about your collection. Tell how you started it, and provide information on the history and development of it. Display your collection or selected items from your collection for the audience to view. This presentation can be held as a service project for a youth center or senior citizens' organization, or you can hold it for friends, neighbors, and other Girl Scouts.

5. Help a group of younger children get started on collecting hobbies. Show them your collection and take them to collection exhibits in museums or elsewhere, if possible. The children may want to begin a group collection of rocks, for example. You can teach them how to identify different types of rocks and help them catalog and display them. You can also take them on a group exploration trip to find rocks.

6. Explore several careers related to your collection. If possible, communicate with people who hold jobs involving your area of interest. Find out what kind of education or training is required. Document your findings.

7. Create a dictionary of terms that are unique to your hobby. For example, if your hobby is stamp collecting, your dictionary will include *philately, plate blocks, definitive stamps,* and *commemorative stamps*. With a rock or shell collection, you would list the different types. Make a cover for your book and illustrate the text. Include blank pages for future additions.

8. Visit one or two museums that have collections. For example, some natural history museums have shell and rock collections. Include, if possible, smaller special-interest museums such as doll museums and fashion, theatrical, or nautical museums. Make an appointment with the curator of the exhibit or somebody else who can provide you with information. Come up with answers to the following:

- How was the collection acquired by the museum?
- How old are the collected items?

- How and when did the collector begin the collection?

- What is the most unusual item of the collection? the most expensive? the most elaborate? the oldest? your favorite?

- How does the collection compare with other collections you've seen?

Prepare and present an oral report to your troop or group on one or more museum collections.

9. Begin a collection of Girl Scout memorabilia. Create a system for keeping track of what you have. You can include uniforms, patches, pins, badges, pictures, swaps (souvenirs that you swap with other Girl Scouts at specific events). Check out local yard sales, flea markets, etc.

10. Explore the world of antiques. Visit several antique shops and see what old paraphernalia you can find at yard sales, flea markets, and even in attics and basements. What items appeal to you? How much do they cost? You can begin an antique collection that includes old jewelry, bottles, sheet music, pictures, postcards, or almost anything.

Creative Cooking

Done

Tantalizing — that's the word for a steaming bowl of soup, freshly baked bread, or a luscious strawberry cobbler. Just as there's more to eating than simply putting food into your mouth, there's more to cooking than plopping a frozen dinner into the microwave. Cooking can be a truly creative activity; it gives you a chance to express your personality and your likes and dislikes.

Like any other skill, cooking requires patience and practice. So what if your first soufflé falls? Next time, it'll be just right and utterly delicious. Good cooking includes menu planning (here's where the real you can come forward), budgeting (knowing what you have to spend and staying with it), shopping (selecting carefully and knowing why), and serving (if the setting looks pretty, the meal will seem more appealing).

Complete eight activities.

1. Save recipes and menus you think you'll like from magazines; newspapers, television, cookbooks, food labels, and restaurants. Don't forget favorites from your neighbors, friends, and family. Start a file of these ideas. Read the recipes carefully, selecting those you feel you are able to prepare and those for which you can easily purchase ingredients. Try out at least one new recipe on your family or friends.

2. Try your hand at several of the following: making yeast or batter breads, biscuits, nut butters, yogurt, cheese, pastry, sauces, or preserves; growing an herb garden or sprouts; drying seeds and other foods; making sausage, deboning chicken, or filleting fish. Don't be bashful about asking for help, especially when you need to use unfamiliar utensils. Share your successes with someone who will enjoy them.

3. Do you know someone you can visit whose kitchen is full of interesting cookware? If not, visit the housewares department of a store or look through the cookware section of a catalog. Ask questions or read descriptions about unfamiliar gadgets. Learn to use and demonstrate your skill with at least three pieces of kitchen equipment you have never used before (for example, a wok, whisk, blender, rolling pin, radish cutter, butter mold, mortar and pestle).

4. Give your meals that added touch. Practice making unusual garnishes, such as chocolate curls, celery fans, vegetable roses, fruit baskets, or fluted mushrooms. Copy attractive garnishes you have seen in magazines, at restaurants, at home, or at your friends' homes. Add these to your recipe file.

5. One trick in good cooking is to start with ingredients that are just right, not necessarily the most expensive. Ask someone to help you know when you are getting a fair deal on good food. Be able to tell how a fresh fish looks, how to choose tender meats, how to pick crunchy salad vegetables or ripe fruits from the market or garden. Read date labels on dairy, bakery, and other products. Describe how a can looks if the food inside is no longer safe to eat. Use this knowledge in selecting food for one of your menus. Or, make a chart to share this information.

6. Using only a camp stove, master a special outdoor cooking technique, such as baking, wok cooking, or steaming. Another possibility is to use a new and challenging recipe on your charcoal grill.

7. Create a menu that requires no cooking, is low-budget, or is suitable for a vegetarian, low-calorie, or other special dietary need. Spark this menu with appealing and nutritious snacks.

8. Prepare a menu for a special occasion with a friend or your family. Serve breakfast, lunch, dinner, or a light refreshment. Keep the following in mind: food availability, eye appeal, cost, balanced food selection, personal preferences, equipment available. Figure out the cost per person for this menu by pricing the items you'll need. Compare prices in at least two types of stores, such as a supermarket, a small grocer, or a produce stand.

9. Invent a recipe. Or, substitute ingredients to improve a recipe you've tried before. Prepare the recipe, keeping track of the ingredients, the quantities, how they were prepared, and the cooking times. Serve your dish to family or friends. Why not submit your recipe to a local newspaper, magazine, special newsletter, or bulletin? You might be cook-of-the-week!

10. Plan a menu and prepare food for a large group (six or more) around a theme for a fiesta, holiday, or special occasion that matters to you. Plan your budget and stay within it as you estimate amounts you'll need for the number of people you'll serve. Make a work schedule of tasks to be done. Decide on table decorations and perhaps some music to accompany the meal. Decide how to do the marketing and how the food will be served. Don't forget the cleanup.

OR

Arrange to take a behind-the-scenes tour of the kitchen in a restaurant, catering business, house of worship, club, school, or camp. Talk to the person in charge about menu selection, food purchasing, responsibilities and training of staff, serving the food, cleanup, or other areas that interest you. Notice how the kitchen is organized and managed to serve large numbers of people.

11. Learn to make a dish requiring a specific technique, such as stir-frying or pastry-making. Take a taste! Are you pleased? How could you improve this dish? Hold a demonstration or a food-tasting party for your friends or your family. Show others how your specialty is prepared, explaining special techniques and/or ingredients. Talk about other menu items that would go well with your specialty.

12. Visit a bakery, specialty food shop, delicatessen, restaurant, or someone's home that has food you have never tasted. Select several ingredients to taste or use in the preparation of a new recipe.

Emergency Preparedness

An emergency can easily become a crisis, if you have never thought about preparing for trouble. Knowing when and how to help is important for everyone — and being prepared is the very first step. You don't suddenly acquire the skills to stop the bleeding in someone's hand, to put out a fire on the kitchen stove, or to protect yourself and others. Simple things, such as a list of phone numbers to call, recognizing the distress a diabetic might be in, or knowing how to turn off the water in your home, may mean a great deal when a real emergency occurs.

By choosing this interest project in Emergency Preparedness, you'll be taking positive steps toward becoming aware of danger signs and knowing how to prevent crisis situations. You'll also learn some skills that will enable you to help yourself and others safely through an emergency situation.

Complete eight activities, including the two that are starred.

*1. Complete a first-aid course and carry a current certification. Be confident that you know how to stop bleeding, give artificial resuscitation, and treat for shock.

2. Make up a first-aid kit to have on hand where your troop or group meets, at home, at camp, or in a car. Include a list of emergency phone numbers and coins for a telephone call. Figure out ways to improvise if you're caught without a first-aid kit.

3. In cooperation with local police and a women's group, plan and conduct a personal security workshop for girls and women in your community.

4. Locate and tour a hospital room, an ambulance, the fire department, the police or sheriff's department, a poison control center, a public shelter, or a rescue unit. Find out how to use these services. Know when and how to report an accident. Post emergency telephone numbers in a conspicuous place at home and where group activities take place.

5. Know the ID disc or Medic Alert identification symbol, the symptoms, and first-aid treatment for medical emergencies caused by diseases such as diabetes, epilepsy, alcoholism, or asthma. Be able to recognize and help someone suffering from drug overdose or withdrawal.

With a parent, guardian, or family doctor, fill out a medical history form or write down your medical history on a sheet of paper. Be sure to include illnesses, allergies, injuries, hospitalizations, immunizations, and hereditary family tendencies. Complete and carry a personal ID card that includes crisis information, responsible persons to contact, phone numbers, etc.

6. Draw up a checklist of household fire hazards. Inspect the place where you live. If you find hazards, point them out immediately and help to remove them. Draw up escape plans in case of a fire in your home. Review and practice the plans with your family, and prepare alternate ways to escape a fire in any part of your home. Know when and how to put out different kinds of fires. Discuss the pros and cons of alarm systems such as smoke detectors.

*7. List what to do in case of crisis. Know what each family or group member should do whenever and wherever an emergency arises. Make a plan for three possible crises that might happen in your community: forest fire, heat wave, cold wave, tornado, hurricane, lightning storm, dust storm, heavy air pollution, volcanic eruption, flood, snowstorm or ice storm, earthquake, tsunami (tidal wave), drought, civil disturbance, riot, power failure, fuel shortage, or nuclear or chemical accident. Seek information from local crisis centers. Practice disaster plans at home. If an evacuation plan is called for, include it in your plan. Give priority to taking care of your need for air, shelter, water, warmth, energy (food), and rest.

8. Learn about the emergency warning signals for your community and personal security alarms for yourself. Figure out ways to get accurate information and send messages in an emergency. Pay attention to how local television and radio stations cover weather news, severe weather warnings, and disasters. Show how you could spread or receive an alarm, call or be called for help, and help stop rumors. If available, check with local ham or CB radio groups and a crisis hot line. Know your telephone company's emergency number. Discuss the emotions that you and others are likely to feel in an emergency and ways you might expect to cope with tension in a crisis. Plan how you might help other people to cooperate and meet the special needs of people with disabilities, elderly persons, and children.

9. Conduct a poison prevention inspection at home. Look for warnings on the labels of household chemicals, such as kitchen and bathroom cleansers, laundry products, cosmetics, medicines, garden sprays, fertilizers, or odor, insect, and rodent controls. Be sure that all poisons, medicines, and alcoholic beverages are out of the reach of young children. Review what to do in case of poisoning. Post the telephone number of the nearest poison control center. Publicize the number in your community.

10. Invite someone from your local health department to talk about the cause, prevention, treatment, and control of a health emergency in your community. Find out what you can do to assist in preventing or controlling a health emergency, such as food poisoning, contaminated water supplies, an outbreak of a communicable disease, severe air pollution, or radioactive fallout.

11. Complete a certified cardiopulmonary resuscitation (CPR) course, perhaps one given by your local Red Cross chapter or heart association. Demonstrate your ability to revive a victim whose pulse and breathing have stopped. Keep your card up-to-date.

12. Know how to turn off the utilities where you live. Ask your parents or the building superintendent to show you how to locate the electrical control panel or fuse box and the water and gas turnoff valves. Learn how to reset a circuit breaker or change a fuse. Practice using a plunger for stopped-up sinks or toilets. Know what to do if there is a gas leak. Collect supplies for emergency lighting, cooking, and water purification.

Family Living

Your family influences you in many ways. Learn more about different family roles, how families communicate, how family life has changed over time, and the pleasures and problems that are a part of family living. You might also want to read the sections "Family" and "Marriage and Parenthood" in the *Cadette and Senior Girl Scout Handbook*.

Complete eight activities.

1. With a group, form a panel and address various viewpoints on issues related to families. Compile a list of issues of interest to your group. For example: Should mothers stay at home when their children are young? How should parents discipline their children? How much allowance should children receive? What is a father's role in child rearing? Each panelist finds information to support a point of view and debates the issue in front of an audience. Let the audience ask questions.

2. Each family has its own system of communication, and it's not just through words. Families also communicate with each other through actions, gestures, and voice tones. With at least one other family member, think of a plan to improve communication and reduce conflict in your family. (Some suggestions: setting aside a regular time to share grievances; finding occasions to give honest compliments or a different way to make requests for favors from other family members.) Together, propose the plan to your family and carry it out for at least a week. If it's successful, consider keeping the new system in place in your family and perhaps even sharing your ideas with others who can also benefit. If your plan did not work out very well, consider devising a new plan.

3. Prepare your family chronology (time line). The chronology can be a collage, a chart, or a tape recording. Include the important events (births, moves, mar-

riages, deaths, etc.) that have taken place since you were born. Highlight the events that caused significant changes in your family. Briefly discuss how these changes were handled. Do this activity with your family and share your chronology with your group.

4. Compile a directory of the services your community provides for families. Include medical, legal, educational, financial, child-care, child-abuse prevention and treatment, and religious services. Provide the address, telephone number, and type of service or program offered. You might visit at least two of these services or write for their pamphlets or brochures. Arrange to have your directory duplicated. Distribute it to families in your community.

OR

Invite representatives from agencies that provide services for families to a troop or group meeting. Have them discuss the type of services provided, the costs involved, and the major family issues challenging that agency. You might also invite parents to the meeting.

5. Find out about the special joys and problems of sibling relationships. Compare three different family situations. For example, you might look at what it's like to be the youngest in a family of five children, how twins relate to each other, or how a sister and brother who are close in age interact. You might want to compare families where there are at least two children with a family with a single child. Once you've decided on three families (one could be your own), observe them several times and keep an observation notebook to record your findings. Notice how the siblings interact, including how they play together, compete, and protect each other.

6. Find out how much it costs your family to run the household for one month. Include costs for food, hous-

ing, clothing, transportation, child care, allowance, and entertainment. List the things you can do to help balance the family budget. Try some of these things for a month and compare the next month's household expenses. Discuss the types of financial problems families encounter and ways to prevent them.

7. Plan a family activity that your family has been wanting to do, but hasn't had the time to carry out. Determine the date, time, place, and cost. Carefully plan the activity with each family member's input, implement it, and evaluate its success.

8. Families vary in size and type. Invite guest speakers to your troop meeting to talk about the different types of families — single-parent families, step-families, foster families, nuclear families, extended families (for example, with a grandparent or an aunt in the household), etc. Discuss these family situations within your group.

9. Find out about the positive aspects and drawbacks of parenthood — how children enrich parents' lives and also change them in terms of careers, finances, social life, and daily activities. Interview fathers and mothers, and include teenage parents. Record your interviews in handwritten or typed form and share your findings with friends.

10. With a group or a friend, discuss and role-play the following family roles:

- a young child in the family who is jealous of a new baby

- a teenager who wants to borrow the family car

- a spouse whose drinking is destroying the family

- a parent who refuses to let her or his teenage daughter go out on her first date.

Think about your past role as a child, your present role as a teenager, and your possible future roles as a spouse and parent. Take turns playing these roles. Discuss the feelings you had and the decisions you were faced with. Make up your own situations.

11. Identify the responsibilities each member of your family has to fulfill in the course of the day. Determine with another family member whether the responsibilities are equally shared and, if they are not, what each of you can do to be more responsible family members. Devise a plan, try it for one month, and evaluate its success.

12. Find out how family life has changed through the years. Talk to individuals of four different ages about what family life was like when they were children. Talk to both women and men. Ask someone who is in her or his twenties or thirties, forties or fifties, sixties, seventies, or older. How do their descriptions compare with what you know of family life today? Document and share your findings with others.

Fashion/ Fitness/ Makeup

Maybe

Did you know that every girl who wishes to can achieve her own personal kind of beauty, physical fitness, and sense of fashion and style? This interest project has been particularly designed to help the "best" in you shine and to assure you that your best is very special.

Looking your best is important because the first impression of the kind of person you are depends in part on the way you look. The visual you is the first thing another person sees. Only later does the inner you become apparent — your character, your intellect, your personality, your values, the health that radiates from you, your warmth and wit.

At this time in your life, your physique and certain systems of your body are affected by changes in glandular functions, causing dramatic spurts in height and weight, the development of breasts, the change in skin secretions (that's why your skin may be oily), and the activation of sweat glands (all that perspiration is perfectly normal). These are some of the realities with which you will work to bring forward the beauty in you.

As you do these activities, you will find ways to maintain good health care, to learn about the proper makeup for you and for the occasion, to stretch your wardrobe, to create your own fashion style, and to stress what is special about you.

Complete eight activities.

1. Determine what skin type you are (oily, dry, combination) and what would be the best way to take care of your skin. Look through teen and beauty magazines, and ask your parents, a local pharmacist, or your doctor to recommend the correct beauty aids for you. Remember that some people — and you may be one — have or develop allergic reactions to chemicals, scents, or coloring in soaps, shampoos, or cosmetics. For example, if you're allergic to cucumbers or strawberries, you'll know you shouldn't use soaps made of these ingredients.

Set up a basic skin-care routine for yourself: cleaning with soap and water, cream, or lotion; rinsing first with warm water, then with cool; patting the skin dry (gently, please); dabbing on a freshener or astringent with a cotton ball. Always give special attention to the forehead, nose, and chin (the so-called T-zone). Consider what particular skin problem you need to care for. For instance, using a medicated soap or liquid with hotter-than-warm water at least three times a day may help control oiliness.

Follow your basic beauty routine for at least two weeks. Note any improvements and any changes you might wish to make. When you find a routine that works for you, stick to it! Then try helping a friend or a member of your group to do the same.

2. Individually, or with one or more group members with whom you feel most comfortable, assess your physical assets and what you feel you could improve. Consider hair, complexion, facial features, body structure, weight, posture, stamina. Write down at least two of your best points and two areas where improvement is needed. Next, plan what you can do to improve things — perhaps a new hairstyle or a daily exercise routine will be good for you. After you've worked on making the "best you" for the period of time you have chosen, look at your list again. Have you succeeded in doing what you wanted to? Is more time needed? Are you ready for another improvement plan?

3. The texture of your hair, its natural wave and growth rate, and your hairline are determined by nature. Everything else is up to you. Keeping hair clean, properly combed, and brushed is among the basics of good grooming. Beyond that, knowing what happens to your hair in rainy weather, in heat and humidity, or in the

cold will help you in handling it in a style most flattering to you.

By looking through beauty magazines, watching television, talking with a beautician or hairstylist, and observing others, decide which of several hairstyles you think would look best on you. Then try one. Keep your new hairstyle for at least a week. (Of course, if you have had it cut, it'll be more than a week!) Are you happy with the way you look now? What modifications would you make? In choosing a new hairstyle, did you change the way you care for your hair?

With others in your group, arrange to visit a local beauty salon. What services does it offer? With the owner or operator, discuss the reasons, both psychological and financial, why people have these services performed by professionals, rather than by themselves. Practice new techniques in the care of hair and nails that you learned from your visit.

4. The growth spurt of teenagers often results in increased weight that you wish would go away. Eventually, it will do just that, as your new body weight is redistributed in all the right places. For now, you might think that dieting is the answer, but crash-diet results are often short-lived. At this stage of your growth, when your body is in a period of rapid development, dieting can do more harm than good. What you may need is a nutritious calorie-controlled routine with your favorite type of exercise that will set good health patterns for you.

Go to your local library and ask the librarian (or your doctor or school nurse) to recommend books written by qualified nutritionists or dietitians. Talk to someone who is interested in nutrition: the home economist at your school, someone in your family, the dietitian at your local hospital. Some of the large food corporations maintain nutrition specialists on staff; you might write to their public relations or customer-service departments for information.

Try to write an eating/exercise routine that suits your very active lifestyle, yet is casual enough to follow and gives you all the vital elements you need for good health. Share your routine with others in your troop or group and with your family. Then, try out this routine for a specified period of time. You may find you'll want to keep it.

5. With two or more people, draw up a list of common myths and realities about health, diet, and your body. For example: Exercise makes you eat more (myth); the use of dental floss is as important as brushing your teeth (reality); breasts can be enlarged with creams (myth).

As a group, collect and read through magazines, pamphlets, and books on the subject of health, diet, beauty, and exercise for ideas to add to your list. Plan a way to put these ideas into action for yourself and to share your newly-acquired knowledge with others. Use print, art, drama, or film to tell others what you have discovered.

6. A wise consumer needs to know exactly what she or he is buying. Research magazine and newspaper advertisements for fashion and makeup. Look at each ad closely to find out what is supposed to appeal to the buyer. Does the ad rely on a personal endorsement (testimonial) from a superstar to sell the product? Or does it convey the thought that "everyone wants to be popular, beautiful, or something you want to be, and this product will make you that way"? Are there disclaimers or health warnings in small print anywhere in the ad? Do you believe what the ad is saying? Try writing a testimonial for a beauty product or fashion item you like and think others would like, too. Present your advertisement and have your troop or group, family, or friends react to it.

7. Learning about makeup — the different kinds, colors, and uses — takes time and practice. Actually, there's no final word on what eye makeup, blusher, lip gloss, powder, nail polish, or whatever, you should use. The color that's best for you is the one that is most attractive on you, that blends with your complexion and enhances your features.

Visit a department store or place where a makeup consultant or cosmetologist works; try to choose a time of day when the store is less crowded. You might be able to arrange this in advance by calling the store. Have the consultant explain the proper techniques of applying makeup and some tips for choosing color tones. With parental approval, one of your group members might act as the model for the cosmetics. Later, try out what you have learned, either individually or with a partner (each girl making up the other). Experiment with different makeup plans for different settings, such as school, a dance, a fashion show, a circus.

8. Being in style doesn't always mean wearing the latest fashions. What you wear in large measure depends on what you're doing, what the occasion is, how much money you have to spend, what you like or dislike. Achieving a personal style is a matter of picking and choosing, of knowing what's right for you — for your age, your build, your complexion. It means adding your own touch — an antique pin you found at a flea market, an old sweater that just happens to match the stripe in your new skirt, a belt your sister gave you.

Collect pictures of the fashion and beauty look you want for yourself; use magazines, newspapers, catalogs, or photographs. You might even be able to attend a fashion show at a department or specialty store. Include ideas for different types of activities and different roles — everyday, informal, formal, indoors, out-of-doors. Choose clothes accessories, makeup, and hairstyles for each season. Compare your fashion look with others in your group, discussing similarities and differences. Save your collection and refer to it when you finish this project. Look at your collection again in a few months. Compare how your ideal fashion image has changed or been modified.

9. By choosing clothes and accessories carefully, you can disguise your figure flaws. For instance, a large waist may mean a long-term exercise regimen and a short-term concentration on loose silhouettes. If you're "too thin," you can add fullness with layers. With heavy hips and thighs, center attention above the waist. Correct posture will help improve your looks and, incidentally, will allow your clothes to hang properly. Make a list of the things you want to cover up by fashion foolery and then search for solutions. Most fashion magazines are a good source to tell you how to do this. Then, in a group, recap the solutions to the figure flaw you each want to play down; refine the solutions to create a look that's all your own. Wear an outfit that reflects the solutions you found.

10. List the things that would make your wardrobe more interesting, functional, protective, or just more fun. For ideas, check out department and sporting goods stores, catalogs, magazines, and books on fashion. Bring one article of clothing or an accessory you rarely wear, a "found" item from a flea market, or something your grandmother may have given you, to your troop or group meeting, or share your item with a group of friends. In teams, put together outfits that include this item. If fit is a problem, you might consider altering or modifying the item to give it a new look. Perhaps you could arrange a clothes and accessory swap or hold a fashion bazaar.

11. From sunbonnets to space helmets, fashion has taken a wayward course, often going backward before going forward again. Explore fashion fads then and now (pick a period that appeals most to you). Books, magazines, thrift shops, and television reruns will give you some ideas of what was fashionable in bygone eras. Collect examples of clothing, accessories, jewelry, and makeup from the fashion era you selected. You might borrow items from relatives or friends, or maybe re-create your own copies. Can you predict what tomorrow's fashion trends will be? Plan a fashion show around your theme of fashion then, now, and tomorrow. Practice wearing and walking around in the clothes chosen for the show. Try to include background music featuring hits of the same era as the clothes each model wears. You might invite girls from other troops or groups, your classmates, or your family to help you plan and to enjoy the show.

12. With today's emphasis on natural products, you might want to try making your own cosmetics. Look through beauty guides, magazines, and books for recipes on how to make facial cleansers, masks, skin moisturizers, skin conditioners, shampoos, and hair conditioners from everyday food products. Some of the items will probably come from your own kitchen; others you may have to buy. Compile a scrapbook of do-it-yourself cosmetic resources for different beauty problems, citing your resources and listing your recipes. Make some of the cosmetics and, with your parents' permission (for safety's sake), try them out. Perhaps you and your group could meet to discuss and exchange recipes and techniques.

Managing Stress

Tension has many sources. It might be the nervous feeling you get when you are about to take a test or compete in an athletic event or act in a school play. Tension is often draining, but it can also be a positive force. It can help ready you for mental and physical challenges.

Each of us has an innate physical response when we feel an overload of tension. This response is called *stress*. Stress can be the result of our awareness of conflicting sides in a situation. It is our reaction to the events around us that causes stress, not the events themselves. We cannot blame ourselves or others for these feelings. They are a result of thought processes triggering physical reactions in our bodies.

This interest project will help you notice the stress signals in your body and learn a variety of ways to manage and relieve stress.

Note: A device is on the market to help you monitor stress. A small adhesive disc attaches to your hand and changes color. This disc can be worn during the day to monitor your reactions to daily activities.

Complete eight activities, including the two that are starred.

*1. Find out how the human body responds to stress, sometimes called the "fight-or-flight" response. What happens to the rate of metabolism, blood pressure, heart rate, rate of breathing, and the amount of blood pumped by the heart? What are the areas of the body to which blood is sent? How would these changes help you get away from a car you saw swerving toward you as you walked on the sidewalk? What happens to the body if it is continually under stress?

*2. To help you identify the sources of stress in your life and begin to deal with them in a positive manner, keep a daily log for one week. Record the times and situations when you feel stressed along with the reactions of your body and your feelings at the time. At the end of the week, review your log and list any patterns you find. Are there any situations you could handle differently to reduce the feelings of stress? A trusted adult or friend may be able to give you some suggestions. Then do one of the following:

Interview five people you know about how they deal with feelings of stress. Are any of their ideas useful for you?

OR

Even in difficult situations, we can sometimes find a ray of hope that prevents us from feeling overwhelmed. Think about five situations you found stressful. Think of a way to bring humor or a sense of hope to each situation.

3. Some of the symptoms of stress can be relieved by physical activity. Fitness, along with getting enough rest and eating well, helps build physical resistance and strength. Make room in your schedule to participate in one of the following activities at least three times a week. Do this for at least one month. Compare how you feel before and after the one-month period.

- Play an active sport.

- Participate in a movement or dance activity that makes you feel more flexible.

- Go for a 20-minute walk, perhaps with your dog if you have one.

- Ride a bicycle for several miles.

- Participate in a vigorous physical activity that lasts at least 25 minutes.

4. Take time to listen to the sounds in your environment. Describe and record the ones you find relaxing and the ones that make you feel tense. Listen to a variety of types of music and find pieces that evoke different emotions in you — happiness, sorrow, anger, playfulness, etc. Record your feelings about each piece of music. Use tension-reducing sounds when you are feeling stressed, perhaps by making a tape recording of your favorite music or taking a walk outdoors.

5. Learning to concentrate your energies on one activity at a time and completing it can help you to manage your time and reduce stress. Visualization is one technique for learning to concentrate. Find a quiet place where you can be by yourself. Sit in a relaxed position. Choose an object or scene to imagine. Try a tree, flower, river, lake, ocean waves, fish in an aquarium, sunset, kite flying, the sky. Clear the rest of the world from your thoughts and try to feel yourself in harmony with the object or scene you are watching. Later, try using your powers of concentration to clear your mind of distracting thoughts and finish a school assignment on time or sharpen another skill.

6. Muscles tense under stress, sometimes without our realizing it. Hunched shoulders from hours of studying, for example, can bring on shoulder and neck pains. Learn to monitor your body and relax tight muscles. You may find a cassette tape with a recorded relaxation exercise on it that you can use. Or you may wish to record these instructions on a tape for your own use. Here is one relaxation exercise.

   • Lie on your back in a comfortable, quiet place. Close your eyes and focus all of your attention on the rhythm of your breathing.

   • Then focus your attention on your lower legs and feet. Tense the muscles in that area and then let them go. Each time you exhale, feel your lower legs becoming heavy and sinking into the surface you are lying on.

   • Now move your focus to your upper legs and buttocks. Tense the area and then relax it. Each time you exhale, feel this area become heavy and sink.

   • Next, move your thoughts to your upper body: trunk, shoulders, head, and neck. Tense, relax, and let these areas feel heavy each time your exhale.

   • Then focus on your arms, from upper arm to fingertips. Tense, relax, exhale, and let your arms become heavy and sink.

   • For the next five breaths, focus on your whole body. Each time you exhale, feel your body relax and let go. Has your body released the tension in the muscles?

   • Relax for several more breaths, stretch, take a deep breath, open your eyes, and then sit up slowly.

Do this each day for a week. Record how you feel at the beginning and end each time.

7. Touching can relieve stress in muscles. Many people like the feeling of a massage — being stroked by the hand. Learn several massage strokes you can use on yourself or a friend to help in relaxation. Try working on your feet, hands, or someone's shoulders.

   For example, a hand can be massaged by making firm circles with your thumb all over the palm. Follow this with circular thumb patterns between the tendons on the back of the hand. Then grasp each finger one at a time with your hand, and with a slight twisting motion slide your hand slowly from the base of the finger to the tip and off. Similar patterns can be used on the feet. A little hand lotion or oil will help to make the motion more soothing. Warm the lotion first by rubbing it between your hands.

8. Keep a diary for one week, recording all the foods you eat and drink each day. Are there foods that make you feel full of energy or nervous? Analyze your food intake each day to see if you eat a balanced diet — foods from each of the basic food groups. Do you eat foods that contain lots of calories, sugar, salt, caffeine, or chemical additives but have few nutrients? Do you eat more or less food than you need? Design a balanced diet for yourself and try it for one week. Record how you feel during this time. Relaxation is important during meals too, so that your body can digest the food. Take time to try out ways to relax and enjoy meals.

9. If you have a problem and don't know how to solve it, try using the following problem-solving process and then learn to make this five-step process for change part of your skills for life.

   • Start with a need, a choice to be made, or a problem to be solved. Write down your goal.

   • List the people who could help you and collect relevant information. Look for alternatives. Write down ways to reach your goal.

   • Consider the information you collected and weigh the pros and cons of the alternatives.

   • Decide on a course of action and the steps needed to make it happen. Act on your decision.

   • Evaluate the results and your effectiveness.

Enjoy your achivement in working toward a solution for the problem!

10. Feelings of stress can be reduced by using the relaxation response. Start by sitting in a quiet, comfortable place. Close your eyes. Relax all your muscles, breathe slowly, and repeat the word "one" each time you exhale. Using a word helps to erase other thoughts that may be racing through your mind. Continue to focus on each exhalation for 10 to 20 minutes. Slowly open your eyes and think about how you feel. Find time to do this once a day for a week. Record your feelings each day and how you feel at the end of the week.

11. There are many family situations that are stressful and leave individual family members feeling isolated and depressed. Divorce, unemployment, drug abuse, serious illness, and death in the family are only a few of these situations. You can be an understanding friend to those you know who are going through hard times, and you can learn how to help yourself if you are going through a stressful situation. Role-playing hypothetical situations may help you to understand the tension created by these problems and to talk about them by sharing your feelings. Role-play the following situations:

- A mother and father are telling their two children that they are separating. The children are concerned about what will happen to them.

- A family attempts to make household budget cuts because a parent has been laid off from work.

- A brother is trying to help his sister, who has been experimenting with drugs.

- Make up a stressful scenario of your choosing.

Exchange roles and repeat some of these situations with different dialogues and solutions.

12. Effective time management is the ability to plan your time and make the most use of it. Such planning often eliminates stressful situations. Create a schedule for a week. Fit in each activity you hope to accomplish from the time you get up to the time you go to bed. Be sure to designate some time to practice relaxation techniques. Create a reasonable schedule for yourself that you think you can stick to. Try it out. What were your results? What did you learn?

Pets

Pets are an important part of today's world. In fact, humans have had pets for thousands of years. A pet is a tame animal that is kept for companionship and enjoyment. Some of the more popular pets are dogs, cats, horses, goldfish, and gerbils.

Complete eight activities.

1. Prepare a care chart on how to care for a specific pet (yours or someone else's) that a pet-sitter could use when the owner is away. Include photos or drawings and specific information that the pet-sitter will need to know about the pet's needs, interests, and peculiarities in order to take care of the animal properly.

2. Find out about the anatomy, taxonomy, evolution, and history of a particular type of pet. Where did it originally come from? Is the type of pet related to any species of wild animal? Was this species of animal used by humans for anything? If so, what? Is this species of animal known for any particular trait? (For example, cheetahs are known for their speed and lions for their strength.) Share your information with someone interested in animals.

3. Learn about the training methods that are appropriate for a particular pet. Develop a training plan to teach a pet two or more new actions or tricks. Find out about conditioning, rewards, and animal intelligence. Show someone what your pet can do.

4. Keep an observation journal on a pet for at least a month. Observe the pet several times each week. Note how it plays, eats, sleeps, and moves. How does it relate to other creatures? What sounds does it make? Find out how these animal behaviors relate to the animal's ability to survive in the wild. Share your information with others who are interested.

5. Teach younger people how to care for their pets. Learn about the care of common pets like dogs, cats, parakeets, canaries, and fish, or others that children in your area may have. After you have done so, schedule, plan, and carry out sessions to help younger children learn how to care for these types of pets.

6. Find out about the laws in your community that protect animals (licensing, leash laws, reproduction and breeding laws, health laws, laws against cruelty to animals). Also, find out which pets are legal and which are not. Share what you learn with others by holding a meeting, making up a booklet, doing a videotape, writing an article, or using any other means of communication.

7. With others who have pets, plan, organize, and publicize a pet show in which owners can show their pets to an interested, invited audience. Have owners highlight the uniqueness of each animal.

8. Shadow a pro. Find out about the careers related to dealing with pets. Spend at least one day with someone in one of those careers or invite the person to tell you about the career if you are unable to be at the site where the person works. Some careers related to pets include the following: veterinarian or veterinarian's assistant; laboratory technician; biologist; naturalist; owners or employees of pet stores; humane society workers; animal trainers; staff of obedience schools, etc.

9. Make the pet's environment as problem-free as possible to help protect it. Research the most common illnesses, problems, and accidents a particular pet may have. Learn the symptoms of these illnesses and problems and how to contact a vet or animal medical doctor. Make a first-aid kit for the pet based on your research.

10. Help pets help people. Research has shown that pets help people in many ways. They provide companionship, help people relax, bring joy, and sometimes even serve as reasons to continue living. Work with a humane society, an animal shelter or clinic, or a veterinarian to help find homes for homeless animals, or working with the same agencies, help set up visiting days for people who are in institutional settings or who live alone.

11. Find out about organizations dedicated to protecting pets. Write to them for information about what they do. Some of these organizations are the A.S.P.C.A., the American Kennel Club, the Humane Society, and the Pets Are Wonderful council. Find their current addresses in the telephone book or at your local library.

Reading

Reading expands your mind and your horizons. Through books, you can explore new lands and people and make discoveries. You will be introduced to new ideas that you can share with others. Reading can change your life by helping you clarify what is important to you. Establishing the good habit of reading helps prepare you for success. So read on!

Complete five activities.

1. Read at least one work from three or four of the following categories: fiction (novels and short stories), poetry, drama, biography, autobiography, mystery, travel, history, and science fiction.

2. Magazines and journals offer interesting articles and stories. Read at least one magazine or journal a week for one month.

3. Reading a newspaper daily is an excellent way to stay informed. Read a newspaper every day for at least two weeks.

4. Meet once a month for at least two months with a group of other readers and have a book forum. Each person tells the group about books she or he has enjoyed reading recently. This is a great way to find out about many different books.

OR

Discuss with a friend or a group of friends each person's reactions to a book that you have all read. Decide on another book to read and then meet again when you have finished it.

5. Organize and carry out a book exchange. The members can exchange books with each other to read and then return them.

6. Organize a read-aloud gathering. Have people read aloud poetry, short stories, or other pieces that they have written or that they have enjoyed reading.

7. Meet with the school and/or local community librarian to organize and carry out a read-aloud program for younger children. Select books for the children's age level and read them aloud to the groups that come to your program. You may also want to find out if your community has access to a cable TV station that can be used to present readings to homebound children. Phone-a-story programs and taped readings are other creative ways of reading to others.

8. Find out what is being done in your community to combat illiteracy. Get involved in the work being done or create your own solutions to the problem. Volunteer at least 10 hours to reading to someone who is unable to read.

9. Find out about *dyslexia*, a learning disability that manifests itself in reading difficulties, and volunteer at least 10 hours in a program serving people who are dyslexic.

10. Find out about careers that involve books, such as publishing, library science, teaching, or book reviewing. Invite a professional to tell you about her or his career in one of these fields. If possible, visit the person at her or his workplace as well.

Skills For Living

Tomorrow — do you really know what it may hold for you? Whatever it may hold, be prepared. Acquiring life skills in personal, money, and household management can help you run your own life smoothly.

You may wear many hats in your lifetime. Whatever lifestyle or combination of lifestyles you choose, being a full-time homemaker or working outside the home full- or part-time, marrying or remaining single, having or not having children, you will need to become an expert resource manager. The day-to-day decisions you make about your own lifestyle have a great effect upon your own well-being, other people with whom you live, and, to a lesser degree, other people everywhere. Be prepared to make informed decisions.

Complete eight activities, including the three that are starred.

*1. Show you are prepared by demonstrating or explaining how to do 10 of the following:

- Report a prowler and report a fire.

- Look up a plumber, a carpenter, utility companies, and a telephone business office in the yellow pages.

- Operate a fire extinguisher, extinguish different types of small household fires, and check a home smoke alarm.

- Regulate heat and know safety precautions for the heating system in your house.

- Change fuses or reset circuit breakers.

- Take care of a stopped-up sink or toilet without using chemicals and fix a leaky faucet. Be able to turn off water in a sink or an entire home.

- Read an electric or gas meter and arrange for telephone service or for the service of one utility company.

- Order a meal in a restaurant and figure the tip.

- Interpret an apartment or house lease or a product warranty.

- Use local public transportation and read timetables.

- Order products by mail, telephone, or personal computer.

- Comparison-shop for three or more items in three types of stores or in three mail order catalogs.

- Replace a broken windowpane or repair a screen.

- Call an ambulance. Handle a case of accidental poisoning.

- Use a self-service gas pump. Change a flat tire.

*2. You're on your own, and the cupboard is bare. Plan well-balanced menus for a first week on your own. Then write a shopping list. You'll need to include the pantry basics you wouldn't have on hand yet (cleaning and paper products, spices, etc.), as well as ingredients needed for your menus. Estimate the total cost, using recent newspapers or by checking prices at the store or on your shelves at home. Look over your list and figure out five ways to reduce the total cost.

3. Inventory your wardrobe and plan what additions or changes may be needed in the next year. What items could you make or remodel yourself? Find out the best time of year to purchase the items needed. Based on your wardrobe, what laundry products or cleaning services would you need to care for your clothing? Show that you know how to make basic repairs (stitch a ripped seam; apply a patch; replace a button), lengthen or shorten a garment, and press wrinkled clothing.

4. Learn life skills on the job or by talking to the pros. Do five of the following:

- Learn how to fill out an application for college or other advanced education and how to obtain an educational loan.

- Compare the services and interest rates at several types of banks.

- Find out what personal and household records should be kept, for how long, and where.

- Show how to balance a checkbook.

- Find out the cost and terms of at least two types of insurance: life, health, car, homeowner's, or renter's.

- Find out how to obtain credit. Compare the cost of at least one large item purchased by cash and one purchased "on time" (using extended credit) or on a layaway plan.

- Find out about several types of loans — for example, loans from a bank, credit union, or finance company, or loans against an insurance policy or mortgage.

- Write a letter of complaint about an actual or imaginary product or service that is unsatisfactory — for example, a new appliance that doesn't work, a repair that is inadequate, an apartment that is poorly maintained or has too little heat, etc. Find out your rights first.

- Find out the refund policy at three types of stores.

5. All work and no play is neither fun nor healthy. See how well you balance your time by jotting down everything you do, and the amount of time you spend on each activity, for at least one week. (Try to select a typical week to do this activity.) Look over your notes and figure out:

- Did each day include some quiet time for yourself? time to exercise?

- Did you spend time doing both quiet and active recreational activities? How could you make time to try something you've always thought about doing?

- Was any time wasted? If so, where and when?

- Did you volunteer any of your time?

- Did the time you spent on school assignments, employment, and household responsibilities allow you enough time for relaxation?

- Where would you like to spend more time? less time? How could you free up or create the time you need?

Make a plan for using your time for another week and stick to it. Compare your accomplishments and how you feel after you use your plan.

*6. There's more to setting up a household than meets the eye. Decide on a type of living situation (apartment, trailer, rented room, house, etc.) and list the essentials needed. Include kitchen items (other than food), linens, tools, cleaning equipment and supplies, first-aid and medical items, small appliances, paper supplies, furnishings, decorations, and entertainment items. Check to see if your list is complete by looking around your home. Estimate the total cost, checking with an adult or using catalogs or advertisements for prices. See how many items might not be needed at all or could be obtained at a lower cost (borrowed, obtained free, homemade, bought secondhand, shared, purchased on sale, etc.). How does this "second look" change the estimated total cost?

7. Running a home is much more than preparing meals and vacuuming. Select at least three adults and find out what they do to keep their household running smoothly. (If possible, include a full-time homemaker and someone who works full- or part-time and takes care of a family.) Discuss the tasks they do in a typical day and the time each takes. Find out if any other person or agency — for example, nursery school, community center, housekeeper, grandparent, or neighbor — helps them perform some of their household/family tasks.

8. Where and how you live affects you in many ways. Interview several young adult friends or acquaintances living in different situations — for example, living alone, with one or more roommates, with family (parents, wife or husband, children, other relatives). With them, explore the pros and cons of each situation. Present your findings to a group.

OR

Think about your values and future goals. Where and how would you like to live? Consider the following:

- the type of housing — a rented apartment or room, your own house, or a trailer

- price and size of the housing

- your own special physical needs

- nearness to work, school, recreation, shopping, family, place of worship, transportation, medical services, etc.

- the type of climate, geography, and setting you would find pleasing

- any other factors important to you.

Try to find out if your dream spot exists. Tell others about your dream spot and why you chose it.

9. Set up a shared household budget for yourself and another person. Start by selecting imaginary occupations for both of you and researching the salaries you might expect. "Select" affordable housing in your area. Decide how much you will spend for other budget areas. Include fixed expenses (rent, insurance, tuition, utility bills, etc.) and variable or day-to-day expenses (food, furnishings, household supplies, personal-care items, clothing, recreation, gifts and contributions, transportation, medical care, etc.). Consider what adjustments you might make if one person was laid off from a job. Check out how realistic your figures are with an adult.

OR

Learn which family expenses are fixed, which ones are variable, and which bills are weekly, monthly, seasonal, or yearly. Help manage the family finances for at least one month. Your activities might include balancing the checking account, paying bills, or keeping track of food costs. Find out what financial records to keep.

10. Plan a cleaning and maintenance schedule for a house or a small apartment. Decide which jobs are to be done daily, weekly, monthly, or seasonally.

   Estimate how much time daily and/or weekly cleaning and maintenance might take you. Try doing two tasks in your own home that you have never done before.

11. Help plan and present a personal household safety workshop. Include how-to's on personal safety in and out of the home and provision for household security while you are away.

12. You've just moved into a place of your own! It's time to invite your family and friends to a party. Plan the invitations, refreshments, entertainments, and decorations for this imaginary occasion. Decide how you would introduce friends from different circles and family members and make everyone feel at home.

Sports

Today, more women are being recognized for their skill and endurance in sports. Through team sports, you'll find out how you and a group of young women with widely different backgrounds can learn to cooperate. Through individual sports, you'll discover how you can discipline and motivate yourself toward a goal. When you play a sport regularly, you'll come to know the pleasure of having control over your body and your emotions.

Participating in, understanding, and appreciating sports can be the beginning of a new you. You'll look better and feel better, too. Even if you don't become a superstar, sports will add fun, excitement, and challenges to your life. The sense of well-being you get from sports will last you a lifetime.

Complete eight activities.

1. Try a sport you've never played before that appeals to you. Learn the rules of the game. Then, watch on television or in person one or more athletic events in the same sport (high school, college, or professional). Decide if professional and school events go by the same or by different rules. Do you see variations in the skills of the players or in the coaching styles? Are various types of uniforms worn or different kinds of equipment used? Make note of these and any other distinctions you have observed during these events.

OR

Compare men's and women's athletic events. Observe a man's and a woman's athletic event in the same sport at the same level, such as at your high school, a nearby college, or in a professional game. Look for differences in the rules of the sport, ability levels of players, coaching styles, equipment, and uniforms worn by players.

2. Write articles for the sports column in a school or a local newspaper or for a sports program. Interview players and coaches for a pregame story. Observe the game and interview players and coaches for a postgame story. Try to make your story sound as exciting as the game was.

OR

Read sports articles in a local or a school newspaper and listen to interviews on television or radio. Figure out similar questions and use them to interview an athlete, coach, sportswriter, or sports commentator in your community.

3. Volunteer for one of these jobs in each of two athletic events: assistant coach, scorekeeper, timekeeper, announcer, photographer, equipment manager, or assistant to the athletic trainer. Prepare for your experience by becoming familiar with the rules of the sport you've chosen and agree on your responsibilities with the people managing the event.

4. Create an international scrapbook of women athletes from different countries and/or ethnic groups. Scan the sports section of newspapers, sports magazines, and athletic journals. Collect articles and photographs for your scrapbook. Choose one newspaper or magazine; compare the number and lengths of articles written on women's sports and men's sports.

5. Read a biography or watch a movie about the life of an athlete or coach. Share the knowledge gained with others in your group.

OR

Become an expert in a specific sport. Explore its history and unique aspects, such as how the sport was developed, what are the basic rules and skills needed to participate in that sport, and who were past and who are present star athletes. Share this information with members of your group.

6. With the help of a coach or physical education teacher, develop a conditioning program designed to improve your level of fitness or to prepare you for participation in a specific sport. Understand the reasons for including each activity in the conditioning program. Decide on a period of time to carry out your program. Compare your level of fitness before, during, and after participation in this conditioning program.

7. Request information on athletic scholarships for women from the Women's Sports Foundation (WSF) or your school guidance counselor. Make a directory of women's athletic scholarships and compare your information with that of others. Share this information with your school guidance counselor and interested members of your group.

8. Make a list of all sports programs and teams open to girls in your community. Be sure to include school sports, both interscholastic and intramural; community recreation programs; and Girl Scout sports programs. Participate in a sport that interests you for a specific period of time. Or, organize a sports program of your own, and recruit players and coaches. Practice, play, and compete with other teams.

9. Select a sport on which to keep statistics of a game or a meet. Learn which statistics are needed and how they are recorded, such as points scored by players and the final score. Observe an athletic event in that sport and keep statistics for the entire game. Compare your statistics with those of the statistician and/or statistics of the game as reported in the sports section of a newspaper.

10. Learn the safety aspects, etiquette, and rules of fair play in a sport of your choice. Observe and follow an official during an athletic event. Then, apply these rules to the sport as an official for an athletic event.

11. Watch a sport that has instant replays on television and analyze the event. Identify skills of individual players.

OR

If you have access to a movie or video camera, film an athletic event. View the film or tape several times to analyze the event and to identify skills of individual players.

12. Choose a sport that interests you or one in which you wish to improve your skills. Enroll in a sports clinic offered in your community or school. Learn the rules, basic skills, and strategies of the sport. Compile a booklet on the sport, including the information you learned, to share with others.

Tune In to Well-Being

Taking responsibility for your own physical, mental, and social health is part of being a young woman. The more knowledge you have about your body, inner self, values, needs, emotions, and strength, the better prepared you are to stay healthy. This interest project will help you to make informed decisions about your well-being.

As you do these activities, you will find suggestions and help for maintaining good health care, eating properly, staying fit, managing stress, protecting yourself, expressing feelings, and relating positively to others. You'll also learn to feel good and be comfortable with yourself.

Complete eight activities.

1. Take a survey of your community to find out what types of physicians and health-care facilities (hospitals, clinics, etc.) are available. Determine what you need to know when selecting a physician or health facility. You might visit a health-care facility, talk with a physician, family members, other relatives, or neighbors. Consider and compare the cost, payment arrangements, location, hours, type of health service rendered, and insurance of a private physician, hospital, and clinic. Share your findings with others.

2. Using the four food groups, prepare a nutritious meal for your family or friends. Include some type of exercise or fitness activity that everyone can participate in before the meal (e.g., jogging, skipping rope, aerobic dancing). Talk about the relationship of diet and exercise to good health.

3. Dramatize or practice with a group of younger children or your peers what to do in each of the following situations:

    • You are caught in a fire in a home, school, store, hotel, etc.

    • You are attacked or robbed on the street.

    • You are being followed by a stranger.

    • You receive an obscene telephone call.

    • You have to report a crime.

    • You are stuck in an elevator.

    • You are approached by a stranger while sitting in a car.

    • You receive a suspicious phone call when you are home alone or baby-sitting.

4. Take a good look at yourself — your diet, fitness level, health, and safety habits. Help become the healthy "you" that you want to be by making a contract with yourself. In your contract, list the improvements you would like to make in order to stay healthy or achieve better health. Sign your contract and carry it out. Plan a way to continue progress in these areas and/or set new goals for yourself.

5. Interview women with various backgrounds in your community and find out what they see as things women in our society are expected to be and do. Try to interview women with traditional and nontraditional views. Based on what they say and from your own observations, create your own collection of expectations for yourself. Repeat this activity to determine your feelings and reactions about role expectations for men. In what ways are they similar to and/or different from your expectations of women?

6. Create a play, game, booklet, puppet show, or slide show to help young children understand the importance of basic personal health habits, such as proper rest, nutritious eating, adequate exercise, brushing and flossing teeth, and cleanliness. Present your play, game, etc., to a group of young children.

7. Stress is an ongoing part of life. The cause of stress can be good or bad. How you handle stress determines whether it is helpful or harmful to you. With another person or a group, talk about the stressful situations you have faced as an adolescent: for example, the death of a close friend or relative, arguments with family members, taking an exam, going on your first date, choosing a college or place of employment. Next, discuss how the feelings of stress have been or can be helpful to you. Become informed about stress management and compile a list of ways to manage stress properly. Be sure to put these ways into action when you are faced with stress.

8. With a group, brainstorm ways in which you might respond when you are at a social event where you are offered drugs or alcohol or where drugs or alcohol are being offered to one of your peers. Role-play the ways you might respond in each situation. Discuss the alternatives for handling the situation and the consequences of each alternative. Which consequences would affect your choice?

9. Compile a directory of human services or programs in your community that provide help to someone who is on drugs, an excessive drinker or smoker, experiencing emotional difficulties, or even considering suicide. Provide the address, telephone number, and a brief explanation of the service or program each agency offers. You might visit at least two of these agencies or write for their pamphlets or brochures. Be sure to include mental health centers, counseling services, hospital clinics, crisis centers, hot lines, health departments, religious groups, and treatment facilities. Distribute your directory to others.

10. Develop your cardiovascular fitness by participating in a vigorous exercise such as jogging, swimming, bicycling, racquetball, jazzercise, aerobic dancing, etc. Participate in this activity two or three times a week for at least one month. Include warm-up exercises before and cool-down exercises after participating in your activity. Also, learn to take your pulse rate before and after exercising. Use a physician, physical education instructor, or exercise instructor as a resource.

11. With the assistance of family members or friends, discover the various ways in which families communicate. Make a list of the positive ways in which your family communicates. Plan an activity that will improve this communication. Carry out your family activity at least twice. Evaluate whether any improvements were made and, as a family, plan a way to make or continue progress in this area.

12. Demonstrate your ability to do at least three of the following:

   • Design a wide game that includes the demonstration of at least ten first-aid skills you have learned.

   • Respond to a medical emergency when you are the first to arrive on the scene.

   • Take your pulse, respiration count, and body temperature and, if possible, your blood pressure. Make a chart of these figures in various situations (for example, resting, before and after exercise).

   • Compile a personal health record, including immunizations, illness, injuries, allergies, and hospital stays. Keep your record up-to-date.

   • Make a personal-care kit and a schedule for its use.

The World of People

Dabbler

What do backpacking along a trail with your troop, participating in an international wider opportunity, earning money for a family whose home was destroyed by fire, and coming to an agreement with your parents about dating, have in common? Each of these activities depends upon your involvement with other people. Anytime you learn more about another person, and put that learning into action, you are exploring the World of People.

Each person in the world is special and all have many things in common. Everyone needs to be loved and to have friends. Everyone needs adequate food, clothing, and shelter. And everyone needs opportunities to learn and to express herself or himself. People have some differences, too. Some of these differences are individual, because each person is unique (there is no one else like you), and some differences are because everyone has a different heritage.

In today's world, people are all very dependent upon other people. The world works best when people can cooperate. Getting along with others means learning to share, to see things from other people's viewpoints, and to work together to get things done.

When you read the newspaper or watch the evening news, do you ever wonder what you could do to help solve world problems? What is your responsibility to the people of the world, or even to those in your community? No one has all the answers, but the more information you have, the more likely you are to make a wise decision. And decision making is part of taking your place in the future.

Service is a way of relating your experiences and knowledge to the needs of others. It is not merely doing something for someone, but helping when and where you are needed. Whether it is in the troop, council, community, country, or world, service has been an important part of Girl Scouting through the years.

So, as you can see, the World of People is your world.

Complete eight activities.

1. Look at your community to find signs of change. What are the population patterns? In what ways has your neighborhood changed? stayed the same? Go to a hall of records, historical society, or library to find out more about the people who settled in your community. Find evidence of their presence in statues, street and business names, architecture, etc. Make a display or produce a pamphlet or newspaper article depicting the things that have changed in your community, as well as those that have not changed, over three or four generations, if possible.

2. Chronicle your heritage by making a family tree. Talk with family members and friends to get all the details. Go back as many generations as you can. Include an explanation of the ways your heritage has affected your lifestyle.

OR

Interview people who are older and compile an oral history and/or pictorial record of their experiences when they were your age. Find out the ways they handled problems similar to and different from your problems.

3. The world is composed of many ethnic, racial, and religious groups. Make a list of everyone you are in touch with on a daily basis. What groups do these people represent? How did each group come to be a part of your community? Find a way to illustrate your community's diversity — perhaps through a food, crafts, or book fair, a play, or a poster.

4. Go to a supermarket, grocery, department store, hardware store, or discount store. Make a list of products that are imported. Check with import-export firms or with government (state or federal) commerce offices and find out what things are exported to other countries from your part of the country. Share your findings concerning the interdependence of the peoples of the world.

5. Find out about international relations as they relate to Girl Scouts. Learn more about the World Association of Girl Guides and Girl Scouts and participate in a Juliette Low World Friendship project.

6. Pick one controversial issue in the news. Read accounts in various newspapers and magazines. Watch television broadcasts and listen to radio coverage. Compare the points of view. Summarize what you have heard or read in the different sources and present it to a group of people through your local newspaper, school bulletin board, or at a community gathering. Ask for reactions to the different points of view. Share your findings.

7. Participate as a nonvoter in an election. You might help with voter registration or provide baby-sitting or other services to make it easier for people to vote.

8. Look at body language. For one day, observe people to find out the nonverbal messages they communicate. Is it possible to say "yes" verbally and "no" nonverbally at the same time? Talk with friends about the messages you convey. Share your findings with a group of people in your place of worship or in Girl Scouting.

9. Try this activity to help you find out how the media affect politics. Look at radio, television, newspaper, and magazine coverage of a political candidate. Listen to or read the verbal message. Try to see the nonverbal message. Think and talk with people about ways a candidate's appearance, tone of voice, or surroundings can affect a voter. Identify ways a candidate is made to look appealing to a voter. Conduct or participate in a campaign for someone in a school election or create a hypothetical campaign strategy for a candidate.

10. Survey your community, decide what needs to be done, and get busy. With a group or as an individual, participate in a social action project. Although service can be given at a hospital, nursery school, or senior citizen's center, try to find other ways to help people. For example, you might provide child care for a mother who needs some time to be away from her family, or you might help in a neighborhood renovation project, or in making a camp or park more accessible to people with disabilities.

11. Look inside yourself for stereotyped ideas you might have about people. Analyze them. Were they based on personal experiences or the experiences of other people? Weigh your emotional knowledge against your intellectual knowledge to find if your feelings have a basis in fact. Look at illustrations in magazines and newspapers for evidence of stereotypes held by others. Create a picture, write a story, or collect news articles to illustrate ways stereotypes can be eliminated.

12. Investigate your legal rights and responsibilities as they relate to civil issues. How old must you be to drive, vote, marry, enter into a contract agreement for credit, or start a business?

OR

Find out your rights as they relate to criminal justice. Talk with a lawyer about the rights of juveniles and how they differ from the rights of adults. Find a way to educate young people about the laws. You might make posters, write a news article, or conduct a law education clinic or mock trial.

American Indian Lore

American Indian tribal customs and culture are part of the rich heritage of our country. They are preserved today by one and one-half million American Indians and more than 300 federally recognized American Indian tribes. They are also reflected in countless place names, foods, crafts, games, and legends that are part of the heritage of all Americans. There are many aspects of this heritage that you can explore through this interest project.

Tribal identity is very important to American Indians, for traditions, cultures, and even languages vary greatly from tribe to tribe. For that reason, many of the activities in this project ask you to learn something about just one or two tribes. Other activities provide an overview of many different tribes. However, you might select one tribe and use it as the focus of all your activities, learning all you can about that tribe. Together, the activities in this project will give you a better understanding of American Indian life and of your own American heritage.

Complete eight activities.

1. On a map of the United States of America, write the present location of at least 25 American Indian tribes or nations. On the map, place the migration routes of those tribes or nations that were forced to move from their original homes temporarily or permanently. Include on your map tribes that were split as a result of being forced to move.

OR

Draw your state map and on it place cities, towns, rivers, and mountains that are named after American Indians or have American Indian names. On your map, place the locations of American Indian tribes or nations presently living there. Then pick a specific time in the past and show where these tribes or nations lived at that time.

2. Learn which plants and animals in your state were or are used by American Indians. These might include crops, plants, berries, roots, fish, birds, and other animals. Find out how the tribes obtained, prepared, and served the food long ago, and whether they still do these things the same way today. Select several traditional American Indian recipes and prepare and serve them to your family.

3. Learn an American Indian craft such as quillwork, silversmithing, beadworking, wood carving, weaving, basketry, stone carving, pottery, or leatherworking. Demonstrate your skill in this craft by making a toy, household article, piece of clothing, jewelry, or art object. Research the methods, materials, and designs so your product is authentic.

4. Read about the history of two American Indian tribes. Select a specific time in history and make a chart to compare the lifestyles of the two tribes during that period. Include the places where they lived, types of dwelling, clothing, food, games, tools, transportation, and type of government. Learn about how these two tribes live today and in what ways their lifestyles have changed.

5. Find out about American Indian games and social or round dances. A place where you might observe those games and dances would be an American Indian powwow, if there is one in your area. Teach two games and two dances that you have learned to a Girl Scout troop or group.

6. Learn 25 words used in everyday life that are derived from any American Indian language. Learn the origin and meaning of 15 states, cities, villages, rivers, or mountains with American Indian names.

7. Talk to members of an American Indian tribe, visit a museum or cultural center that has a display on American Indians, or visit an archaeological site that has evidence of an American Indian presence. Make a cassette tape, an album of photographs, or a scrapbook of drawings to show what you learned about one American Indian tribe during this visit or talk.

8. Read two treaties or agreements made by the government of the United States with American Indian tribes or nations. Find out when and why two different tribes were forced to live on reservations.

9. Select a period in time and study the designs of dwellings and villages of several American Indian tribes during that period. Then, using clay, papier-mâché, cloth, or other appropriate material, build an authentic model of a dwelling used by one of the tribes. Write a description of how the dwelling would be furnished and how it would be used.

10. Read stories about six American Indians who played an important role in the history of this country. Tell which tribes they are from. What is the basis for their fame? What effect did they have on the history of this country?

11. Become more knowledgeable about American Indian legends, myths, and folklore. Focus on one tribe and find out if that tribe has legends that can be told only at certain times of the year. If so, learn the reason for this tradition. Be sure to respect this tradition when requesting to hear legends or when telling them.

Visit an American Indian cultural center or museum to hear or find out about some of the legends.

OR

Read several American Indian legends that are authentic. Design some illustrations for one or more legends to be used in telling the legends to younger children.

12. Look through books or view films or television programs that feature or include American Indians. Try to locate illustrations, photographs, film clips, and scenes that are supportive, positive, and accurate descriptions of American Indians. Also watch for pictures and words or phrases that include inaccuracies and stereotypes and could be considered offensive to American Indians. Discuss your findings with a group and share your feelings about what you found.

Community Time Capsule

Did you ever stop to think that the past shaped the present, and that what takes place today in a community will influence its future? In fact, the community in which you live is a time capsule — full of information about people, places, and things. Do some digging; find out where your community has been and where it is going. You'll make discoveries about yourself, your neighbors, and the past, present, and future of your environment. And you'll be preparing for leadership.

Complete eight activities.

1. Listen to old records or rereleased versions of old records. Locate sheet music of popular music at least 15 years old. Learn three dances or songs that were popular in the past. Hold an "oldies, but goodies" dance contest or concert. You might wear outfits that were fashionable when the music was a hit.

2. Find out how teenagers dressed during three different periods in your community's history. Include clothing, makeup (for girls), and hairstyles of all cultural groups. Hold a fashion show or an exhibit of different styles of dress. Explain what the styles indicate about being a young woman or a young man at different times. What sorts of activities were encouraged or discouraged by the types of clothing worn? What messages were people getting about women and men from the way they dressed? Did these messages differ among various cultural groups?

3. Produce a portion of a newspaper as it might have appeared in your community 60 years ago. Include such items as controversial topics of the time, advertisements, and business information.

   For resources, talk with people and/or read reference copies of your local newspaper. Look at early mail-order catalogs. Use your 60-year-old newspaper to advertise the events in the first or second activity in this interest project. Write a similar newspaper for the year 2020.

4. Interview people representing the diverse groups in your community about the lives of women and men approximately 25 and 50 years ago. You might ask: What was expected of girls and women? What work did they do? How did their lives differ from those of boys and men? What were families like and what were family members expected to do? What was education like? dating? marriage? child care? What changes have occurred in the community? Which changes were brought about by technology, such as new machines to speed housework, and which by social change, such as a family's need for increased income?

   Find a way to share this information with others. You may want to make a display with pictures of the people you interview, make a tape recording or slide/tape program of the interviews for a local historical organization, or write a newspaper or book to record this oral history permanently.

5. Identify events that you feel had an important effect on your community such as the building of a new dam, highway, or shopping center, population growth and change, industrial changes, the civil rights movement, the Great Depression. Find out the extent to which your community has changed and why. Describe your findings through a painting, photography, a film, a short story, or a play. Make your art form available to your community as a whole, or to a religious, neighborhood, school, or youth group.

6. Investigate your community's natural history. Find out how geographic features such as mountains, plains, waterways, and lakes have affected your community's growth. Join a group or design a project yourself to help preserve your natural heritage. You might restore a park or garden, clean up coastal lands or a parking lot, or make an educational display or presentation concerning natural preservation in your area.

7. Interview people who have moved to your community, bringing with them different customs, traditions, folk art, languages, or ways of dress. Find out why they came and how they got there. What problems did they face by coming to a new community? What were the strengths they brought with them that helped them in their new community? What traditions have they kept from their old lifestyle? What changes have they made? Share what you have learned with a community, school, or Girl Scout group.

8. Compile a songbook, crafts book, cookbook, or book of folktales representing your region of the country and its cultural, racial, ethnic, and religious heritages. Gather ideas and information for your book from neighbors, family, and other local residents. If more than one language is commonly used in the community, you might prepare a bilingual or multilingual book with the help of translators.

9. Talk to representatives of different religious, ethnic, and racial groups to find out how their group contributed to your community's art, architecture, food, music, poetry, prose, film, business, technology, agriculture, and community service groups. Share what you have uncovered in your investigation in a program such as a community dinner, a film or music festival, or through a community guide or photography display.

10. Conduct a heritage hike in your community. Visit landmarks and trace contributions made by people of various national origins, with different jobs or ways of life, or from different racial, ethnic, or religious groups.

11. Volunteer at a local museum, community group, or historical society working to preserve your community's heritage.

OR

Individually, or with your group or friends, help restore a building or some artifact from the early days of your community.

12. Project what you think your community will be like in 10 or 20 years. Talk with members of planning groups, school boards, community groups, human rights groups, urban renewal agencies, and service clubs. Also talk with public utility officials, business people, and others about their predictions and plans for the future. Do you agree with their visions?

Explore the use of laws in helping communities now and in the future. What needs to be done today to protect your tomorrow — ecologically, in terms of transportation, energy, school, business, industry, and housing?

Will life in your community be improving or not? Give form to your new ideas and feelings by putting your vision for the future into a drawing, photography exhibit, map or model, a story or film, a news article, or a community action. Show what you can do to contribute positively to your community's future.

Do You Get the Message?

Do you get the message when "hearing" body language? Do you say what you mean and mean what you say? This interest project will help you explore the many ways we send and receive information.

Complete eight activities.

1. Much of our daily communication is unspoken. Begin tuning into nonverbal communication by playing a game of charades. Follow up on your exploration by keeping score while watching a sports event on television with the sound turned off. Now, observe person-to-person interaction in public places, such as libraries or transportation waiting areas. With a partner, observe nonverbal communications for fifteen minutes. Note how attitudes, moods, and emotions are communicated through body language and facial expression. You and your partner record your findings separately and then discuss them.

2. Learn a little of a language that is new to you. Be able to communicate six short phrases in your new language. You might choose Braille, sign language, Morse code, a foreign language, or a computer language. Visit a site where your new language is used and try your skill or teach your new language to a friend or a group of younger Girl Scouts.

3. Many people receive the majority of their current-events information from television, with radio and newspapers being secondary sources for news. To discover more about what is involved in news reporting, do the following: With two or more people, monitor a news story as it is reported in two or more different media (television, radio, newspaper, magazine). Compare how the story is told, the way words are used, what the pictures show, and the point of view of the news source. Rewrite the coverage of one news story to show a different point of view. Share both stories with a group.

4. With a group of at least four, form two teams and take opposite sides of an issue affecting your community. After each team investigates all the factors that support its side of the issue, debate the issue before an audience. Allow the audience to vote as to which side was more convincing. Record your findings and, if possible, share them with community leaders.

5. Did you ever think about what you purchase and why? Explore the ways that advertising influences our lives. Choose three products that you use frequently: for example, shampoo, toothpaste, cosmetics, detergents, cereals, etc. Spend one week noting the ads (TV, radio, magazine, newspaper) for your products. Then answer the following questions about the ads for each product:

   • What promises are made about the product?

   • What was used to get your attention (music, color, headlines, familiar voice, etc.)?

   • In visual ads, how were the models dressed?

   • What ads made you want to buy the product?

6. Design an imaginary product (either a new one or an improvement of an existing one) and develop an advertising campaign for it. Create posters, slogans, jingles, etc., to describe the product and encourage its use. Present your ads to a group and find out if they would be persuaded to buy your product. Discuss with the group what parts of the campaign appealed to them, and why.

7. One of the most effective tools of communication is the written word. Practice expressing yourself through one of the following:

   • Keep a daily journal (or diary) of your thoughts and feelings for two weeks. Include what happened in school, at home, and with friends.

   • Write an account (fiction or nonfiction) of an incident involving someone your age.

- Interview someone older than you (parent or friend) about a school or work experience the person had at your age. Write the story she or he told you.

8. How does clothing "speak"? Find out by exploring some of the ways that communication is affected by what the communicator is wearing. Look through magazines and mail-order catalogs to see current trends.

    Design a costume to communicate each of the following messages. The costume designs may be sketches, pictures cut from magazines, doll clothes, or actual garments. They might include clothing, shoes, hairstyle, makeup, and/or accessories.

    - I want to be noticed.

    - I want to relax.

    - I want to blend into the crowd.

    - I want to impress someone.

    - I don't care what people think.

    Share the designs with a group. See if they can "get the message." Find out if different people received the same messages. Could the messages be misinterpreted? Do clothes make the person?

9. Which is more important, what you say or how you say it? Explore the effect that tone of voice and mannerisms have on verbal messages. Pick a neutral sentence, such as "It is cold today," and say it in a way that would express four different emotions, for example, anger, love, impatience, nervousness. Be sure to include body language, facial expressions, hand motions, etc., that also convey the emotion. Role-play in a group to see which is louder, the verbal or nonverbal message. For a week, analyze your verbal and nonverbal messages. Are you "saying" what you mean?

10. Choose a comic strip to follow for two weeks. Decide whether a message (political, philosophical, etc.) is included or whether the strip is used to entertain, or both. Create a comic strip, funny poster, joke, skit, or story to tell a message. Share it with someone for her or his reaction.

11. Explore the messages that physical surroundings can communicate. Look at several room designs in homes, schools, public buildings, stores, museums, or magazines. Note colors, textures, furniture, and use of space. Design a floor plan or model room for two of the following:

    - a children's dental clinic

    - a hospital waiting room

    - a student lounge at a school

    - your private space

    - a Girl Scout service center.

    Share your design with others. Did the messages you wanted your design to convey come through?

12. Write a résumé that accurately conveys your school and work experience. Design an outfit for a job interview and practice interviews for two or three jobs listed in the classified pages of the newspaper, or use your résumé to get an actual job interview. Practice verbal and nonverbal communications before the interview.

Games

People have enjoyed games for thousands of years. There are card games, board games, electronic games, target games, tile games, outdoor games, indoor games, and all sorts of games! Through games, people find pleasure, challenge, relaxation, friendship, and opportunities to develop and practice skills.

Complete eight activities.

1. Learn to play at least one game that you don't already know from *each* of the following categories:

   • card games (e.g., old maid, gin rummy, poker, solitaire)

   • board games (e.g., checkers, chess, backgammon, Monopoly)

   • electronic games (e.g., computer games, electronic toy games)

   • target games (games with targets: e.g., darts, marbles, horseshoes, shuffleboard, tiddlywinks)

   • tile games (a game in which tiles are used: e.g., mah-jongg, dominoes, Scrabble).

2. Learn and play five games that require cooperation among the players. Teach these games to others.

3. Find out about the history of various games. Discover how these games reflect the cultures in which they were created. Share what you learn with others who are interested in games.

4. Learn four games that are popular in other countries. Teach them to others.

5. Teach younger children three games you liked the most when you were their age.

6. Find out what a wide game is and plan and play one with others.

7. Invent your own game. Teach it to and play it with others.

8. Find out about careers that involve games. These careers may include the following positions: recreation specialist; physical education teacher; simulation game leader; coach; therapy and fitness center leader; camp counselor; toy/game designer, manufacturer, or salesperson. Invite people in these careers to speak with you and others who are interested. If possible, spend a workday with them.

9. Young children enjoy circle games (games played in circles like "Duck, Duck, Goose," "Ring-Around-the-Rosy," "Hot Potato," "Little Sally Ann"). Find out about circle games and teach them to and play them with Daisy or Brownie Girl Scouts or other groups of young children.

10. Plan, publicize, and carry out a game party in which friends can play games from various categories. Include board, card, tile, target, relay, and circle games and other games you enjoy.

11. Challenge your logical and creative abilities by doing six word games or mathematical puzzles.

12. Discuss the different feelings that winning and losing games cause in participants. Do reactions differ for games of skill and for games of chance? Think of ways to help players realize it is *how* you play the game that counts.

Global Understanding

Without people, would the world be quite the same? People, after all, are an important part of anyone's life — yours, too. And the fascination of meeting people, of any age, from other backgrounds, other races, other cultures, other countries, other religions, adds to the richness and joy of life. What do you imagine someone from another country would think of you? Are you curious about the lives of young people in other nations?

The more people know about each other, the better their understanding and goodwill. Since all understanding begins at home, so to speak, you can start by defining the values (what people consider important) and lifestyles of your own community. Then, watch your knowledge grow as you delve into this interest project on Global Understanding.

Complete eight activities, including the one that is starred.

*1. Your reactions to people and things are very often influenced by your own perceptions and the milieu in which you live. Try to look at your community through the eyes of someone living in another country. Put together a scrapbook, pamphlet, slide show, or multimedia presentation that answers these questions about your community for this person. Include examples from all groups represented in your community in your presentation.

   • How do people earn a living?

   • How is family life affected by the ways people earn their living?

   • What is family life like? How are love and affection expressed among family members and friends?

   • How are the lives of boys and girls similar? How are they different?

   • How has life been changing in your community?

   • How do people in your community view themselves and others?

   • Does their religion influence their behavior?

   • What do people in your community enjoy doing?

   • How do people in your community define the "good life" — a life worth living? How is your community working to make the good life accessible to all?

   Use the resource you developed in one or more of the following:

   • a tour of your community for people from another country or community

   • a bilingual or multilingual program

   • a citizenship class

   • a gathering for people who are unfamiliar with your community, such as international visitors or travelers from another part of the United States

   • a program to prepare girls or adults for travel outside the community

   • a community display located in a bank, library, house of worship, or community center.

2. Prepare a list of international resources in your community. Your list might include people, organizations, businesses, and shops. Use your list to do at least one of the following:

   Help Brownie or Junior Girl Scouts have an international experience. For example, meet people who are citizens of, or who have lived in, another country; organize an international fair or a games or crafts day;

carry out international activities for Brownie Girl Scout Try-Its or Junior Girl Scout badges.

OR

Help a hostess receiving visitors from outside the country. You might help that person learn more about a guest's country, customs, and daily living habits.

OR

Assist people planning a trip abroad by telling them about the resources in your community — people and things — to help them plan their trip.

3. Become a walking resource on another country or on an ethnic, cultural, racial, or religious group represented in that country. Be able to answer the questions in the first activity for the country you choose. You can get these answers from people in your community who have lived or traveled in that country; from pen pals; from your own travel experiences or those of relatives; from books, magazines, newspapers, filmstrips, films, and television.

4. Plan and stage an event where each participant wears women's clothing representing a different country or ethnic group. Discuss what that clothing tells you about being female in the country or group, the modesty expected of women, and the activities women can comfortably do; and what effect this garment has on the way you move, behave, and work.

Find out what clothing young women in a country of your choice wear to school, on the job, on special holidays.

OR

Compare the latest fashions for men and women in a country of your choice or for an ethnic group of your choice with the traditional national or ethnic dress.

OR

Compare women's and men's clothing in a country of your choice.

5. Prepare an entire meal from another country or region of the world. Serve and eat the meal as people from that country or region might, following their customs and etiquette. What does the meal tell you about the nutritional habits of the people and the land, waters, climate, and economy of the country or region?

6. Learn a performing or visual art typical of another country. Consider what makes the art form typical and why it does or doesn't appeal to you.

OR

Express a familiar experience or a common emotion in an artistic way that is typical of another country. Some forms to try are poetry, painting or sculpture, dance, music, or drama — for example, haiku poetry of Japan, shadow puppets of Indonesia, or masks of Africa.

7. Make a model or detailed drawing of a home outside the U.S.A. Include furnishings, pets, garden, etc. Be sure your house reflects the climate, family structure, beauty, and technology available in that country.

8. Experience in person, or through a book or film, a celebration of something important to young women in another country or culture, according to the customs of that country or culture. Consider: naming, coming of age, graduating, marrying. The celebration should show something about family values and the culture's expectations of women.

9. Find out about a religion that differs from your own. You might choose to learn about the predominant religion of another country or about a religion in this country. If possible, visit a house of worship of this religion in your community, and/or talk to someone of this faith.

   Share with others the specific ways the religion affects the values and lives of the people. List adaptations you would make in living and/or eating habits if a person of this religion visited your home or school.

10. Find out if people in your community are getting fair and accurate information about the politics and the social and financial conditions of people in other countries. First, decide on a country. (You may use the country you chose for the third activity or any other country for which you can answer most of the questions in the first activity.) Then, do one or more of the following:

   • Conduct a poll or series of interviews with students and friends. Ask them to describe their understanding or impressions of that country and its people. Compare their responses with what you know.

   • Watch a television show or a film or read about this country. Compare the way the people are depicted with your own understanding of them.

   • Follow a news issue related to that country. Check television, radio, and newspaper reports. Decide whether or not you feel the coverage is accurate and fair. Explain why or why not.

   • Get copies of textbooks used in your community's schools. Look at the treatment of that country, illustrations used, information emphasized, values and customs highlighted. Decide whether or not the textbooks are giving an accurate, up-to-date, and fair picture of the country to students. Be able to explain your decision.

   Compare your findings with others in your group and decide whether or not your community is getting accurate and unbiased information about countries around the world. If not, you may want to organize a special project in your community to see that people are better informed. You might write letters to the editor of your local newspaper, or send a spokesperson to a radio or television talk show.

11. Inform yourself about a global issue affecting people in your community and in communities around the world. Hunger, energy, pollution, health, human rights, multiracial understanding, or housing are possible topics. See whether any organizations in your community are working to lessen the problem locally or internationally. If so, spend some time assisting one of these organizations with its projects.

OR

Design a community project to help your community deal with a global issue.

12. Interview one or more people whose careers have a global reach, such as employees of international businesses and service organizations, diplomats, travel agents, importers, exporters, translators, or tour guides. Design career cards for these careers. Include photographs and information from an interview, job descriptions, special qualities needed on the job, salary, places of employment, and sources of additional information.

OR

Hold an international career night. Have a roundtable or panel discussion with some of the people mentioned at the beginning of this activity.

Heritage Hunt

Exploring your "roots," learning and sharing your own cultural heritage, helps you and others see how important your background is. The influence your family and other people have on your community is significant, too. Then there is your community's heritage — rich, varied, and changing through the years. Is this heritage documented and well-preserved, or is it being lost through neglect or beneath the wrecker's ball, housing developments, or shopping centers? You may be able to assist in documenting, maintaining, or preserving the heritage of your family, people, and community.

Complete eight activities.

1. Ask your family members or older members of the community to tell you stories of their lives or stories they have heard told in their families. Compile an oral (tape-recorded) history and/or a pictorial history of these stories and share it in some special way with members of your family or community. You might do this by donating copies of what you have compiled to your local library or historical society, interesting your library in having an oral history section, or encouraging your historical society to start an oral history project if it doesn't already have one.

2. Construct a family history chart — a family tree — for yourself or someone you know well. Where possible, include the full name, maiden name (for women), and the dates and places of birth, marriage, and death of each person listed on the chart. Go back as many generations as you can. Begin with what the family members and family friends can tell you. Find information in birth, baptismal, marriage, or death certificates, the family Bible, etc. When you have finished, make copies of your work for interested family members and/or your local library, historical society, or genealogical society.

3. Choose a woman of the past whom you admire or find especially interesting and learn all you can about her. She can be one of your ancestors. Find out about her

family, friends, and community. Using all you have learned about this woman, write a biography or make a scrapbook that would be representative of her life.

OR

Locate the oldest tombstone you can find in an old local cemetery or at a historic gravesite. Find out all you can about the person whose grave it marks by talking to longtime residents or looking through historical information in the library or in historical society records. Use courthouse records or census information to help you in your research. Explain to others what you have learned.

4. Family traditions are often observed at special times in our lives — birth, coming of age, marriage, or holidays. What family traditions do you observe? Ask your family members for help. Talk with them about which ones you like (or dislike) and decide how you can pass them on. Prepare a food that is a specialty and/or favorite of your family. Share it with your Girl Scout troop or group and, if possible, explain how it came to be a family tradition.

5. Learn all you can about your own roots and heritage. How does your cultural background affect your life with respect to food, celebrations (birthdays, weddings, holidays), family get-togethers, child-rearing practices, education, recreation, dating, engagement, marriage, and/or jobs? Spend some time talking with older family members or older friends of the same background about your cultural traditions.

OR

Plan a project to increase community awareness and pride in your cultural heritage. Examples of such a project might be a neighborhood cookbook or songbook, a block festival, a series of newspaper articles, or an exhibit at a fair or in a library or mall. If possible, compare your findings with someone in your troop, school, or neighborhood who shares a common heritage with you.

6. By using old maps of your city, town, or county, U.S. Geological Survey maps, or aerial photos — or by talking with senior citizens, morticians, or stone carvers — search out the locations of old local cemeteries. Locate as many as you can and mark them on a current map. Present the map as a gift to your local library or historical society.

OR

"Adopt" an old cemetery of special interest to you or your troop or group and assist with its maintenance.

7. Locate an old work site, such as a mill, factory, lumberyard, mining operation, blacksmith's shop, train depot, canal locks, wharf, fishery, farm, or ranch. Find out all you can about how the work was carried out at that particular site by researching old newspaper accounts or, if possible, talking to former owners or employees or their descendants. Find out about such things as the safety factors involved, the hours worked, details of the jobs done, and for indoor sites, such as a factory, what the lighting and ventilation were like.

Take someone on a tour of the site or design an exhibit of your findings, using drawings, photographs, or artifacts, for display in a public place such as a store window, museum, library, or fair.

8. Make a collection of pictures of old buildings in your community or local area. Include single- and multiple-family dwellings, religious buildings, work sites, barns and silos, and outbuildings such as springhouses, milk houses, root cellars, or bake ovens. Choose one building and learn all you can about it — its architecture, its use, its former inhabitants.

OR

Assist in a restoration effort for a historic building.

9. Search out information about your community's heritage. Who were the first people to live in your community, town, city, or county? When did various waves of settlers arrive? When was the area incorporated? Did it have any reorganizations or boundary changes? What have been the special events in its history (influential visitors, celebrations, wars, buildings erected, highways completed, etc.)? Using the answers you have found, make a time chart or display to illustrate your community's lifeline.

10. Do two activities young women of previous generations would have done as part of their everyday lives. Teach one to younger Girl Scouts or do a third activity. Here are some possibilities; you may think of others.

- Bake bread and make butter.

- Learn to spin on a drop spindle or spinning wheel and to finger weave on a loom.

- Gather the necessary natural materials and learn to dye cloth with them.

- Forage wild edibles with a naturalist or other trained person and prepare and eat what you gather.

- Plant an herb garden. Learn the uses of these old plants for medicinal purposes as well as for cooking, and learn any legends and superstitions about them.

- Learn how to chop and split wood, square or hew a beam, or refinish a piece of wooden furniture.

- Learn to prepare, from scratch, foods common to your area such as sauerkraut, scrapple, succotash, corn bread/johnnycake, fish dishes, etc.

11. Make a model or floor plan of a typical house or multiple-family dwelling in your community 100 years ago. Include furnishings, garden, outbuildings, and neighboring buildings.

OR

Make comparisons between your home today and a home 100 years ago. List everything in your home today that did not exist 100 years ago. Beside each item write its historical counterpart. Share with someone the contrasts you have found.

12. Learn about solar energy, combustible fuels, wood stoves, food storage, methods of dress, transportation, etc., in earlier times that could be used efficiently today. Prepare a written, illustrated, or oral advertising campaign to persuade people to adopt an old method that is practical today and conservationally sound.

The Law

As you move through the day, laws play an important role in your activities. Whether going to school, shopping, riding in a car, watching television, reading a newspaper or book, or just talking on the phone with friends, you are affected by many different kinds of laws. Each of the activities mentioned above is controlled, governed, protected, or regulated by law. Schools have compulsory attendance regulations, shopping involves contracts and commercial standards, passengers in a car are protected by standards and regulations for both driver and car, television has guidelines set by the Federal Communications Commission, newspapers and books are protected by the Bill of Rights, and telephone communication is governed by rules that both you and the phone company must follow. If you would like to learn more about the fascinating subject of the law, this interest project is for you.

Complete eight activities, including the one that is starred.

1. Investigate how laws are made. Be familiar with the process of lawmaking on a federal, state, and local level. Find a law that interests you and trace its history by finding out when it was enacted and why it was necessary.

*2. Find out about the rights of young people. For example, when do youths become adults in the eyes of the law? Find out about the laws that govern your right to vote, to operate a motor vehicle, to attend school, to seek employment, and to obtain credit.

3. See the law in action. Observe at least two of the following proceedings in your area (obtain permissions if and where necessary):

   • a school-board meeting that involves voting

   • a town/city council meeting

   • a criminal court trial

   • a civil court trial

   • a session of the legislature

   • a special court session (e.g., juvenile justice, landlord/tenant, small claims).

   Share your findings with a group of younger children.

4. Find out about the people who make various kinds of laws, interview two of them, and trace their career paths. Check with the following:

   • city/town council members

   • judges

   • city manager

   • legislators

   • school-board members

   • lawyers.

   Have them talk about their jobs, educational backgrounds, and community experiences. Find out how they think their jobs affect the community. Share what you have learned with others in your troop.

5. Before a proposed bill becomes a law, the legislature holds hearings where the public can present their views on the proposed action. Hold a mock trial or mock commission hearing on an issue of your choice. If you choose a trial, have others act as judges, jury, lawyers, plaintiff, and defendant on a civil issue that is facing your community. If you choose a mock hearing, select an issue that is currently of concern in your community. Have people participate on both sides of the issue.

6. Who are the people that ensure compliance with the vast number of rules, laws, and regulations in our society and communities? Ask five people (guidance counselor, teacher, etc.) to discuss with you the different types of law enforcement careers on a local, state, and federal level.

7. The Constitution of the United States established government under law. Become familiar with the U.S. Constitution and the rights, duties, and powers it confers. Follow the events surrounding a current constitutional issue as reported by the news media. Keep a journal describing the events and your reactions.

8. Why is voting so important? Be an advocate for voter registration in your community. Volunteer your services to a nonpartisan voter registration drive.

9. Write a play, skit, or story, or produce a video for a young audience, dramatizing what can happen to a juvenile who breaks the law by shoplifting or driving while intoxicated or using a controlled substance. Research the details so that they are accurate. Interview people who work within the juvenile justice system. If possible, produce your dramatization for a group.

10. Choose an issue in your community (school, neighborhood, or community at large) that needs addressing. Get involved, research the issue, find out its pros and cons, then inform your community about what you have learned. Help organize a panel discussion or a young peoples' forum on the subject.

11. Write a letter to your elected representative (federal, state, or local), newspaper editor, or local television station expressing your opinion on any issue (homelessness , hunger, teen suicide rate, etc.) that is plaguing your community.

12. Some laws are designed to protect the civil rights of all people by preventing discrimination based on a person's racial or ethnic background, disability, or sex. Investigate the 1964 Civil Rights Act, especially Title VII, as well as Title IX in the Education Amendments Act of 1972. What rights do these titles or acts protect?

Leadership

Leading a group of any kind is a skill that can be learned, practiced, and improved upon. Essentially, being a leader means being responsible for taking a group from one point to another — that could be as simple as walking from here to there safely, or as complex as resolving a serious conflict within a specific period of time.

Your Girl Scout council is a good example of an organization that helps girls and adults develop leadership skills. Through training, special events, outdoor activities, workshops, and committee meetings, girls and adults have the opportunity to try leadership roles.

How about you? Does leadership of a group sound appealing to you? Is it something you're unsure about, but would like to try? If so, then this interest project is just right for you.

Complete eight activities, including the three that are starred.

*1. List the strengths you bring to your group. Use the list opposite "Things a Leader Does," or design one of your own, based upon your ideas and observations. This list will help you identify leadership abilities you have, those you want to improve, and new ones you would like to develop.

2. After receiving permission to act as an observer, visit two consecutive meetings of at least two different groups, such as a Girl Scout council committee or a council board of directors, women's or men's service group, community planning board, PTA, Daisy, Brownie, or Junior Girl Scout troop or group, senior citizens' club, board of education, religious group, local grange, city council.

Before your visit, talk to the group leader about the group's interests and the activities planned for each meeting. During the meetings, look for leadership skills and action in the group. Notice how people interact by asking yourself questions such as these: Who talks and why? Is there a balance of participation? Should there

be? Who helps move the group along? Who blocks progress? Why? How does the setting (room, tables, lighting, etc.) affect the group? Does the leader get everyone involved? Are goals stated? clear? worked on? achieved? If you did this activity with others, talk over your observations.

*3. Through real-life situations or role playing, show that you are able to help a group do each of the following:

- make a decision

- make plans to reach a goal

- work in partnership with people of different ages, races, ethnic groups, cultures, or religions

- resolve an argument or difference of opinion

- evaluate your progress in a task.

*4. Through research or by talking with others, make a list of the qualities of a good discussion leader. Then use these guidelines as you lead each of the following:

- a discussion to share ideas, feelings, experiences, or information about an issue important to the age group you are leading

- a discussion to arrive at a decision or to set goals

- a discussion of various sides of a controversial issue

- a discussion to evaluate projects.

Have each group plan what it wants to accomplish and when and where. As the leader, demonstrate basic techniques for starting a discussion, sharing responsibilities for decisions, sticking to the topic, seeing that everyone has an opportunity to be a part of the discussion, and closing the discussion.

5. With other project members or adults, agree on a list of three or four situations that a leader might face in working with a group. You choose the group. Take turns acting out ways you would respond, as a leader, to each situation.

Things a Leader Does

	In past leader-ship situations I have done this *(check each statement that applies).*	I plan to work on this *(check each statement that applies).*

Helps People Work Toward Goals and Do the Things They Want to Do

	In past leader-ship situations I have done this	I plan to work on this
Gets things moving	_____	_____
Helps the group:		
• set goals	_____	_____
• make decisions	_____	_____
• choose directions	_____	_____
• evaluate progress	_____	_____
Suggests solutions and ways to get things done	_____	_____
Provides books, information, equipment, etc., to help with a project	_____	_____
Helps coordinate the parts of a project	_____	_____
Guides the work and efforts of others toward their goals	_____	_____
Shares skills and know-how	_____	_____
Helps others develop their skills as leaders	_____	_____

Helps a Group Get Along As a Team

	In past leader-ship situations I have done this	I plan to work on this
Helps people get at the causes of problems	_____	_____
Helps group members understand one another, keeps lines of communication open between members	_____	_____
Helps resolve differences, disagreements, conflicts	_____	_____
Helps group morale, encourages with a sense of humor	_____	_____
Helps each group member use her talents and interests to be part of the group's action	_____	_____

Helps a Group Keep Up Momentum and Move Ahead

	In past leader-ship situations I have done this	I plan to work on this
Helps or gives direction in emergencies	_____	_____
Knows and helps interpret rules that apply to the group	_____	_____
Helps group keep an eye on progress	_____	_____
Teaches others how to lead	_____	_____
Helps group discover new interests and directions	_____	_____
Supports and encourages	_____	_____

What Other Kinds of Things Do Leaders Do?

_____

_____

_____

_____

_____

6. Demonstrate your knowledge of the basic rules and steps for each of these methods of group decision making: (a) formal voting with parliamentary procedure, and (b) deciding by consensus.

7. Select one or more persons you would like to interview on the topic of effective leadership. Prepare a list of questions that you want to include in your conversation. Contact the person(s) and arrange an interview. After your discussion, share your findings with others who might be interested in leadership — for example, with your project participants or through an article in your school newspaper.

8. With a partner or on your own, create a plan for improving some working procedure or method of operation that is currently used in your school, religious group, Girl Scout council, job, or community. Clearly describe the following: the situation as it is now; why improvement is needed; how your plan would improve the situation.

    Take your plan to the person(s) who can improve the situation. Work with them; persuade them to adopt your plan.

9. Teach someone else how to do something you do well. Also, learn a skill from someone else. In a group, share your thoughts about both situations. Start your own lists of tips for teachers and tips for learners. Try out your tips as you become involved in other teaching or learning situations.

10. Do one or more of the following:

    Assist an adult leader of a Brownie or Junior Girl Scout troop for at least three meetings.

    OR

    Help an adult leader of a Brownie or Junior Girl Scout troop prepare for its first camp night or outdoor experience. If possible, go with the troop.

    OR

    Lead at least three sessions of a group of your choice: for example, your school or religious group, a community group, a group of older adults, a neighborhood play group, a day camp, or a hobby club.

11. Identify an ongoing need (recycling waste, building school spirit, preventing child abuse, aiding people with disabilities, expanding Girl Scout membership, etc.). Recruit or join others to work together on the project. Show leadership by promoting a positive image through posters, presentations, news items, or other means.

12. Direct a project or task group with members your own age. Plan your work by identifying goals and ways to accomplish them. Construct a time line to chart your work, assess your progress as you go along, and evaluate your final results.

Travel

Done

Going somewhere — whether it's around the corner or around the world — can really be an adventure. Travel means all sorts of marvelous experiences, people familiar and new, breathtaking sights, and exciting things to do. Your imagination is your ticket to anywhere, but travel takes planning and that's what this interest project will help you do. For starters, borrow and study your leader's copy of *Safety-Wise*. Read the chapter, "Planning Trips with Girl Scouts." Then make sure all your real travel plans conform to your Girl Scout council's travel procedures.

Complete eight activities.

1. Spend an hour or so on a round-trip travel adventure in your community. Go with the idea that beauty can be found anywhere. Along the way, open your eyes and ears to sights and sounds that are beautiful or unusual to you. Take pictures, make a tape recording, draw a sketch, write a poem, or just keep a record of something you have seen for the first time or in a new way.

2. Soon you will be of voting age and can participate as a voter in your city, state, and federal government — one of the rights and responsibilities of citizenship. To observe your government in action now, you might visit your mayor's office, a local courthouse, your city or town hall, your state capital, or Washington, D.C. Arrange beforehand to talk to an official or an aide while you're there. You may want to follow up with additional visits and interviews.

3. Take a trip wearing a blindfold or earplugs to help you understand the problems faced by someone whose sight or hearing is impaired. For safety's sake, be sure to take a friend along to help you. Reverse roles with your friend so you also can practice ways to be helpful.

OR

Working together with someone who has a physical disability, find out what needs to be done to make a specific place accessible to that person. Share your findings with your community.

4. Use a map or chart to guide you on one of your travel adventures. Show that you can follow a road or street map, a subway guide, or a bus-route map. You might want to consult a topographical map for hiking, a nautical chart for traveling by water, an aeronautical chart for traveling by air, or a tourist's guide to a museum or park.

5. Choose a theme for a tour through an area in or near your community. Plan your route, including places of interest. Seek some information about these places. Arrange to take a group on your tour; afterward, ask what highlights appealed to the group.

6. Make it easier for people who may find travel difficult on their own. Invite a person or a group, such as small children or older people, to share an adventure with you. Prepare them beforehand for what to expect and set a pace to meet their special needs. For example, plan a train trip for a nursery school group, a day-care class, or a Brownie troop or group. Accompany the group and their teacher or leader on the trip.

7. Venture out by land, air, or water, using different types of transportation. You might "go public" and take a train, a ferry, a taxi, a bus, or a commercial flight. Other ways might include going for a sleigh ride, a sail, a canoe trip, a horseback ride, or a bicycle ride. Use at least two modes of transportation and then make some comparisons. How did your travels differ in speed, comfort, fun, cost, convenience, time schedules, reservations, or other ways?

8. Try seeing your community through the eyes of an international traveler who knows only a few words of English. Figure out how you would get from place to place, order a snack or meal, and find toilet facilities. Look for signs that don't translate easily, such as

"powder room," "soft shoulder," or "hot and cold heroes." Learn to recognize universal signs or symbols and encourage their use in your community. Find out about difficult adjustments to life in the U.S.A. by talking with students from other countries, immigrant families, religious groups, business persons, or local organizations that assist international travelers. Do something in your community to make these adjustments easier.

OR

Enjoy dining out. Make reservations to eat at a restaurant where the menu includes foods that are unusual to you. Determine what you should wear and what are considered good manners. Order a meal, and include something you've never eaten before. Handle paying the bill, and leave a proper tip.

9. Find out about jobs that have to do with travel. Contact someone who travels on the job or whose work has something to do with travel. You might talk to a travel agent; sales, delivery, or repair person; harbormaster; road-equipment operator; toll collector; state police officer; tour guide; civil engineer; air traffic controller; airline employee; bus or train dispatcher; officer on a ship or plane; or others you know. Ask about the nature of their jobs, personal qualities or preparation necessary, and advantages and disadvantages of the work. Record the information. You may use the format in *From Dreams to Reality: Career Cards.*

10. Where would you like to travel? Choose two places. Gather information about ways to get there. Find out about special rates and discounts, as well as extra charges for services you might want. For example, how much would it cost to take your pet? Figure economical ways to include travel gear and equipment. Compare the costs of renting or buying things like skis, bicycles, camping gear, a van, a boat, a backpack, or luggage. Keep a file on your findings and make it available to others.

11. Decide when it's best to take a suitcase, a pack, a duffel, or a handbag. Show ways to save space and select items for multiple use. Make a list of often forgotten items. Figure out ways to improvise or make substitutions for things you left at home. Practice taking care of and keeping track of your things so they stay neat and won't get lost. Finally, carry all your baggage around for 10 to 15 minutes to make sure you can handle it easily.

12. Plan a trip you intend to take in the United States or to another country. Help yourself by using the skills you've learned in the other activities of this project. Use travel guidebooks, brochures, maps, and advice from other travelers to help you plan your itinerary. Estimate costs, including transportation, living arrangements, food, and sightseeing. Learn about the buying power of a dollar wherever you'll be and how to exchange money if you're going out of the U.S.A. Take care of required paperwork, allowing plenty of time in your planning to obtain medical clearances, and get passports and visas for international travel. Before you go, find out what's special about the place you plan to visit. Keep a daily journal or take pictures while you're gone; when you return, look back at the things you enjoyed most. Write down any ideas you want to remember for future travel.

Understanding Yourself and Others

Are you curious about other people — about why they do and say certain things? Do you want to learn more about yourself? By doing this interest project, you'll have the opportunity to see how special you are, set and work on personal goals, learn how appearance can influence others, develop ideas to help people make better use of machines, change people's attitudes about important issues, and help your younger Girl Scout sisters deal with the peer pressure they will experience.

Complete eight activities.

1. Teenagers often say, "Nobody understands me." Put together a booklet to help parents, teachers, and other adults gain a better understanding of what it means to be a teenager today. Use cartoons, photographs, poems, stories, etc., to get your viewpoint across to adults. Share your booklet with an adult close to you.

2. Set a personal goal and try to achieve it by following the steps outlined in the section "Reaching Your Goals" in the *Cadette and Senior Girl Scout Handbook.* Decide and work on a goal that you can reasonably accomplish in a month.

3. The way you act is often influenced by your attitudes — your thoughts and feelings about an issue. Design and carry out a project to change attitudes, and hopefully behavior as well, about one of these important issues:

   • drunk driving

   • seat belts

   • racial or religious prejudice.

   Remember, attitudes are often emotional and deeply ingrained. Presenting a good, logical argument may not be enough to change people's attitudes.

4. Role-playing is a valuable technique that allows people to become more sensitive to and aware of another's point of view. Each participant plays the part of an individual in a specific situation. With friends, role-play at least two of the following situations:

   • a girl wants to meet the new boy in class

   • a girl is being pressured by her friends to try drugs at a party

   • a blind girl joins a Girl Scout troop or group

   • a girl makes a prejudiced remark about a classmate who is not there

   • a girl's parents tells her she can't go to the school dance.

   Each situation should be role-played for 5 to 10 minutes. Spend some time afterward discussing your feelings and evaluating the exercise.

5. Every culture develops social norms or particular ways of interacting with people (such as how close people stand to each other when they're having a conversation). Find out what happens when you break these norms by doing one of the following:

   • Go to a public place, such as a library, and sit right next to a person who is at a relatively empty table.

   • During a conversation with a friend, stand closer to her than you usually do.

   • Ride an elevator facing the back instead of the front.

   • Treat someone whom you're usually friendly with in a formal manner (for example, call her Mrs. Brody instead of Marsha).

   How difficult was it for you to do the activity? How did the other person(s) react? Why? Find out about some social norms in another culture.

6. Write your autobiography, describing the one most significant event from every year or two of your life. How do you think these events have affected you?

7. Any time people get together is a good time to learn about them. Have fun learning about people by having a people-watching party. Invite a variety of people — if possible, people from different backgrounds, of different ages, and boys as well as girls. Observe body language (gestures, facial expressions, posture, etc.) and what people say to each other. If you can't give a party, people-watch at a mall, in a department store, or at some other site.

8. Peer pressure can be a powerful influence in a girl's life. With some friends, put on a play for younger girls that demonstrates both the beneficial and harmful effects of peer pressure. Read the section "Peer Pressure" in the *Cadette and Senior Girl Scout Handbook*.

9. Find out how clothing makes a difference in the way you feel and act and the way you are treated by others. How do you feel and act when you wear your Girl Scout uniform? Do your friends, classmates, family members, neighbors, and strangers treat you differently? What happens when you wear casual clothing? fancy or formal clothing? Keep a record of your feelings, the way you act, and how others react to you as you change your style of clothing during a two-week period. Observe how you react to people wearing various types of clothing.

10. In many instances, people get hired for jobs because of their ability to understand and get along well with all kinds of people. Employees also get fired because of personality conflicts with supervisors and coworkers. Interview three people who hold different types of jobs and observe them at work to see for yourself how important "people" skills are in a work setting.

11. Accidents are often caused by "human error" (for example, pressing the wrong pedal in a car). Some of these mistakes might not occur if tools and machines were easier for people to operate. Change the design of a tool or a machine (such as a car, a computer, a garden tool, or a household appliance) to make human errors less likely. People who do work in this field are called "human factors engineers." If you come up with a really good suggestion, send it to a manufacturer of the product.

12. Everyone plays many roles. You are a student, a Girl Scout, a friend, and so on. List all of your roles. Do the same for an adult you know. Spend a full day with the adult you've chosen so you can see how that person acts as she or he goes from one role to another (for example, from work supervisor to coworker to mother to wife and so on).

13. Find out how well television represents old people, women, and people of color. For a one-week period, keep a record of three shows that you watch regularly, including the commercials throughout the shows. Pay attention to what each character is doing (for example, cooking dinner, walking a dog, or working in a lab), the personal attributes (intelligence and attractiveness, for example) of each character, the job each one holds, how important each character is, the family situation each one is in (for example, married or widowed), and how each character is treated by others. Draw some conclusions from your observations.

Women's History

Could you be a detective or an investigative reporter? Try this interest project to find out. In these activities, you'll search for information about the past roles of women, write about the accomplishments of women, and think ahead to your own future in the twenty-first century.

Complete eight activities.

1. Explore your personal history by finding out about the women in your family. Look back at least two generations by reading family records or by talking to relatives and record important events in the lives of women in your family. Did those events reflect what was happening in the world at that time? How did the women's lives reflect their personalities, values, and family traditions? Record your findings on audio or videotape.

2. Survey at least 12 children's stories or nursery rhymes and songs that have female characters. Look for the ways women are presented. Discuss these characterizations with another person. Decide ways you could counter negative or reinforce positive images.

3. Create a resource file of women's achievements in the history of your state. Include information about women from different racial and ethnic backgrounds. Organize your resource file and make it available to school or community groups.

OR

Research the United Nations Decade for Women and the three meetings connected with it. Find out about the strategies developed by the U.N. to improve the lives of women all over the world. Share your findings with your community.

4. Compile a history of the last 30 years from women's perspectives. Interview at least six women of different ages about their opinions and experiences concerning world and national events.

5. Find out about the contributions of North and South American, Asian, European, and African women in a variety of fields (e.g., arts, science, government, sports). Your exploration may center on contemporary women or women from the past. Use your findings for a fun presentation and share it with younger children.

6. Talk to a professional in the legal field about state laws that affect women. For example, what are the laws concerning child custody and support, the owning of property, and the ability to obtain credit? Have the laws changed since 1960? What changes would you like to see made in the laws? Find out the procedures in your state to change the law.

7. Find out about child-care options for working women in your area. Compile the information into a directory and make it available to the women in your community.

OR

Learn how child care has changed in the last 50 years. Research and write a history of child-care choices.

8. Attend meetings of organizations founded by and for women — for example, your local Girl Scout council, the Young Women's Christian Association, Women in Communications, and the League of Women Voters of the U.S. Find out about their histories and their services for women and the community.

9. Interview women in leadership roles in your Girl Scout council. Compare their education and their personal and professional backgrounds to determine characteristics that have helped them to develop leadership skills.

10. Help a group of younger girls to explore women's history. Help them find and use resources that tell about the contributions of women. Lead them in a discussion of the impact women have had on the history of this country and the world.

11. Organize or participate in an event to honor the contributions of women; for example, a women's history fair, a women's film festival, or an awards program to honor the contributions of women in your community.

12. Write your own personal history. Include your education and your goals, as well as information about your family. Include women who are your role models and why. Be sure to include the ways your experiences in and out of Girl Scouting have influenced your goals.

The World of Today and Tomorrow

Dabbler

The World of Today and Tomorrow is the realm of new frontiers. It is knowledge, creativity, energy, and change. Whether it's a new business practice, the latest discovery in the natural or physical sciences, a new tool to revolutionize industry, or a just-discovered way to harness energy, the latest news will be old news tomorrow. Science, mathematics, technology, business, and industry have unlimited potential for the future. Creative minds are changing the world around you in everything from cooking to communication.

Your energy and imagination are needed in these exciting times. The possibilities are endless. New horizons can open as rapidly as today's laser travels to tomorrow's space station. Your ideas may be the ones needed to open up a new and better life for everyone.

Complete eight activities.

1. Follow the path pollutant oil takes into the waterways. Because most oil pollution in America's waters comes from vehicle engines and not from major oil spills, use discarded car motor oil in a simulation. First you fill a large glass jar with layers of sand. Add layers of gravel, fine stones, soil, and crumbled plant material. Then spread the oil over the top of your "ground." Periodically, "rain" on your ground by sprinkling the jar with water. Record what you see happening to the oil after one week, six weeks, longer. Try varying the combinations of layers. How does oil reach streams, rivers, lakes, oceans?

   To properly dispose of the oil, put the contents of the jar into a bucket with lots of warm water and some dishwashing liquid. Stir this all together and then pour off the water into a sink. Return the soil to the environment. The detergent should help disperse the oil into small droplets that can be further broken down as it travels through a waste-water treatment plant.

   OR

   Find out how jetties, breakwaters, bulkheads, and dams affect the flow of water and the materials it moves. Make drawings or take photographs to show how these structures have directed the flow of water, sand, and other materials.

2. Try your skill at being an animal trainer. A family pet may be ready for a new trick or perhaps you can start with a different animal, such as an insect, frog, or fish. Make absolutely certain you know the food and home needs of your animal. Decide carefully what you will teach and how you will reward. Find out about your animal and be reasonable in what you expect. Always treat your animal in a kind and humane manner. Some ideas to start with could be having your animal run a maze, respond to a signal, find a hidden object, or perform a new maneuver. For one month, keep a record of your training progress. Compare this exercise with your own learning experience. Do you see any similarities? any differences?

3. Can you be a weather forecaster? Do you know what the weather map in the newspaper or on television is really indicating? Find out the meaning of the symbols used on such a map, how high and low pressure areas, direction and speed of winds, temperature and land features affect your weather. Track at least two storms as they form and move across a part of the earth. From what you see happening with these storms, predict what will happen in your area as other storm systems start. Check your forecast with the actual weather.

   OR

   Collect or make your own weather instruments. Keep a record of the weather for several weeks and compare your readings with the official ones in your area. Find out about the very sophisticated equipment a meteorologist would have.

4. Design, plan, and construct something you or someone else can use. Once you know what you want to build, your first and most important step will be to do a rough outline of your basic design. Try to experiment with various shapes and sizes. Use the sketch to do a scale drawing of your design.

Whether it is a storage chest, doghouse, horse stall, platform bed, or another item you are making, be certain you have precise measurements because this plan will determine the type and quantity of the materials you'll use. You should know the length, width, height, and area dimensions to determine the amount of building materials, such as wood, paint, glue, nails, etc., that are required. Investigate different kinds of materials as alternatives; for example, plywood versus wooden boards, or stain instead of paint.

You should know your options, so shop around and compare prices. Use your imagination; a clever idea can substitute a less costly item for an expensive one. Decide when quality justifies the expense. Your final choice will depend on the amount of material you'll need, the overall design, and your budget. Build your piece. Keep track of all your plans and figures so you can compare your finished product with your original plan.

OR

Become an expert at scoring a team sport, such as bowling or softball, so you can keep important statistics for the team, such as individual and team batting averages. Act as a scorekeeper for a school team, recreation commission team, or other team.

5. Long ago a town crier walked through a town and shouted the news. Today there are many ways to tell people what is happening in the world. Visit a newspaper printing office, telephone company, radio or television station, or a school business office near your home and find out how information is collected and shared. What equipment is being used? How has the equipment changed during your lifetime? Find out what changes are now being made in the way this facility communicates. Design a futuristic way to spread the word to your friends or someone far away. Share your design with others through words and drawings.

6. Be able to maintain and do safe simple repairs on one or more of the following:

   • bicycle, car (change tire, lubricate)

   • faucet (change washers)

   • lamp/electrical plug (rewire)

   • power lawnmower (change oil, clean and set the gap on the spark plug)

   • sewing machine (clean and lubricate)

   • window (recaulk, replace broken pane of glass).

   OR

Try one or more of these do-it-yourself ideas: Assemble a piece of technological equipment, such as a radio or telescope, with a kit or your own materials. Design and construct a model of a bridge or building structure. Learn how to operate a home or small business or school computer.

7. Plan and carry out an expedition, overnight if possible, to explore the night sky. If you make certain you have a clear night, you should be able to see many different things. Observe as many of the following as possible: a planet, meteor, your zodiac constellation, stars of different colors, an artificial satellite, the North Star. Plan ahead and try to be out on a night during a special celestial event, such as a lunar eclipse, meteor shower, comet appearance, or special planet grouping. Take a telescope or binoculars to aid in viewing. Make a record of your exploration.

8. With a group, create a marketable product using the individual skills of each person. You might make food, clothing, a household item, holiday decorations, or gifts. Keep track of the money needed for your raw materials. Use advertising techniques to market your product in your community. Sell your product or make it part of a money-earning event. Assess the important needs associated with running a business — investment, productivity, marketing, and profit-making — and the satisfactions and frustrations of business life.

9. Assemble or build your own kite. Experiment with your kite to find out how to control it and which winds are best. Modify your design to make it fly better. Enter a kite-flying contest or festival, or organize one of your own in your community. Find out about kite flying or kite fighting in a country other than the United States.

10. Put on a chemical magic show to entertain a group of people. Look up some interesting and colorful experiments in a "how to" book on magic. Try to find at least three tricks that involve a bit of chemical magic. Be sure you can explain "what's happening" to the audience.

11. Conduct an archaeological investigation. Archaeology is the scientific study of the remains of historic or prehistoric peoples and their cultures. It includes examining their living areas, tools, clothing, writing, and other remains.

    Try to find an archaeological site to investigate. Visit a prehistoric site to collect information or see if you can join a "dig." If this is not possible, visit a site of historical significance, such as a house, factory, or town square constructed at the turn of the century or earlier. Obtain important information by checking courthouse records and by interviewing older people familiar with the area. Take photos and record interesting features about the site. You might like to write a short story about one day in the life of a past inhabitant of your site, or recreate a past skill or craft, such as dyeing, tool making, or a recreational pastime.

12. Grow an improved seed. Through genetic research and technology, most cultivated fruits and vegetables are now superior to those grown 50 years ago. Get some new hybrid and/or disease-resistant seeds and cultivate a "superplant." If you don't have garden space, grow your plant in a large container. Scan a seed catalog and find out what other varieties of your plant can be grown. Share your findings and your crop with your troop or group, friends, or family.

OR

One concern today is to make certain there is enough nutritious food for all the people in the world. Find out as many different ways to get nutritious food as you can. Select at least one way and see how the process for getting, preparing, or preserving this food, and/or taking it to market has changed in the past 10 years. Some food sources to consider are the following: raising pigs, chickens, or cattle; growing grain or fruit; or harvesting fish, seaweed, or other food from the water. Share this information with your troop or group or another interested group.

Audiovisual Production —Basic

Recent technological advances have brought more options and possibilities to audiovisual production than ever before. Only a few years ago, film and videotape were separate and distinct fields, computer graphic capabilities were limited, and digital technology was unheard of. Today, the competent AV producer must be familiar with a wide variety of technologies and the techniques for using them, either simply or in combination.

If you are a newcomer to audiovisual production, this interest project will help you learn something about the various technologies available and become familiar with the skills that go into producing quality AVs.

Complete all of the activities.

1. *Planning the audiovisual.* The most important question to ask yourself when planning an audiovisual is, "What's it for?" In other words, what do you want to communicate to whom? This question must be answered before you begin thinking about medium (film, videotape, slides, etc.), length, or technique. Once you've identified your audience and your message(s), then you will be able to plan the other aspects of your AV.

   Research the characteristics of at least three audiovisual media. You might choose slides, videotape, motion picture film, audiocassette, or computer graphics, among others. Decide which medium would be best to use for a specific purpose, such as a training AV for younger Girl Scouts about cookie sale safety or an AV to inform parents about Daisy Girl Scouting.

2. *The team.* Many special skills and talents go into producing a single audiovisual. A team of professionals usually includes a producer, director, scriptwriter, narrator, on-camera talent, and technical personnel such as cameraman, video engineer, and lighting director. Sometimes, one person will fill more than one job, such as director/cameraman or writer/producer. Nevertheless, AV production is always a team effort, so the ability to work together is critical to the success of your project.

Find out about the major jobs in AV production and the skills, education, and experience necessary for each. Then, interview an AV professional from your community. Find out her/his experience, professional background, and what she/he thinks is most necessary for success in the field. Good interview candidates can be found at area TV stations, cable operations, colleges, and some high schools. A local still photographer or the photo editor of your local newspaper would also be a good subject, as would a radio disc jockey.

3. *The business of audiovisuals.* A great deal more than creativity goes into producing a successful audiovisual. A production needs funding, for example, and budgets must be developed. Contracts must be written and signed. A production schedule is important too, as are legal releases from the cast and permissions to use existing visuals or music. For professional AV productions, the producer usually handles these tasks, or a business manager may be assigned.

   Research the current federal copyright law. Find out how to copyright an AV that you produced and what "public domain" means. Imagine that you are producing a video for your favorite popular song. Find out who owns the song (usually not the singer) and draft a letter to the owner asking for permission to use it. Be sure to include information about how your music video will be used.

4. *The audio.* There are various audio production techniques (live script, recorded audio track, music, etc.) that can be used in an AV. The visual portion of the AV must be compatible with the audio, so a script must be limited to those subjects that can be economically illustrated.

   Watch three different audiovisuals, such as a television program, an information film in school, or a Girl Scout video from your council. Make notes on the type of audio that is used and give some thought to why it was chosen to deliver a particular message to a particular audience.

5. *The storyboard.* A storyboard is a scene-by-scene drawing of the AV plan. Its upper portion illustrates what the visual will be for a given scene; its lower portion shows what audio will accompany the visual. The timing of the audio and the video for each scene is precisely the same. Sample storyboards may be found in any good book on AV production; check your local library. Also, an area TV station or advertising agency may be willing to provide you with sample storyboards from actual productions. Study these storyboards and then create your own storyboard for a short slide show, videotape, film, or television program.

6. *Locations and casting.* A shooting location is the best place to get the visuals you need for a particular audiovisual. A casting session helps you recruit the best group of people to appear in the AV. Both the location and the cast must be carefully selected if your AV is to deliver the message you want.

   Select a favorite novel, play, or short story and imagine that you are making a film of it. Choose well-known actors and actresses to play the major roles and have at least two reasons why you selected a particular individual for each part. Then, choose locations in your area that you think would be good places to shoot your movie. Have at least two reasons why each location was selected.

7. *Production.* The word "production" refers to the stage in AV development where the actual shooting of visuals and recording of audio takes place. This is the time that the storyboard is put onto the selected AV medium, whether it be color slides, videotape, or motion picture film.

   Observe a production in either of the following ways and try to identify key production staff, including the director, the cameraman, the script monitor, and the producer.

Observe an AV shoot in a studio or on location. If there is a TV station in your area that generates local programs, ask if you can attend a taping. Many nightly news shows are broadcast live and offer an excellent opportunity to witness studio production, provided the station allows visitors during these broadcasts.

OR

If you are unable to view a production firsthand, try watching a documentary about the filming of a movie. Most video stores rent cassettes on the making of films or music videos.

8. *Postproduction.* This is the stage when all the elements of the AV are put together into the final product. Slides are sorted, cropped, and paired with an edited audio track. In film and videotape, images and sound are edited together and special effects, if any, are added.

   Observe one of the following at work: a film editor, a videotape editor, a sound editor, or a still photographer selecting slides. Video and sound editors can be found at most TV and radio stations. Depending on the size of your community, there may be video or film production facilities that will allow you to visit. Find out why a particular slide or video scene is selected by the editor. Interview the sound editor to discover what makes one audio segment superior to another. Find out how sound effects or special visual effects are added to a production.

9. *Evaluation.* Critically review a TV program, movie, or slide show. What do you think its purpose is? Did it meet its purpose? What could be better about it? Write down your reactions to the production. Then ask two friends to independently review the same AV. Compare your evaluations, noting the differences in your comments. Try to decide why different people view the same AV in different ways.

Audiovisual Production —Advanced

If you have completed the Basic Audiovisual Production interest project or have acquired equivalent audiovisual production experience in some other way, you may want to do the more advanced activities described below. These activities are aimed at helping you produce your own audiovisual.

Complete all of the activities.

1. *Planning the audiovisual.* Develop a written proposal for your own AV. Include its purpose, its basic message(s), its audience, what medium you intend to use, and where you intend to show the AV (in a school auditorium, on home video, etc.). Your choice of medium depends on where the AV will be shown. Also include the basic technique(s) you will use to convey your message. For example, you might produce a music video to convey an antidrug message to an audience of preteens. Or you might put testimonials from current Girl Scout leaders on a videotape that will be used to recruit new leaders.

2. *The team.* Put together a production team for your audiovisual. Choose people who have different strengths and skills. A person who enjoys creative writing might be your scriptwriter, for instance, and someone who has a resonant voice your narrator.

3. *The business of audiovisuals.* Develop a budget and production schedule for your audiovisual. In the budget, you may need to include the following: the cost of blank videotape or film, snacks for younger children appearing in the AV, the cost of photocopying the script, film developing, and local transportation costs, among other items. Depending on your particular situation and the type of AV you are producing, some of these costs will be eliminated and others will need to be added.

For your production schedule, estimate how much time it will take to complete a given stage of production. For example, how many days will it take to shoot the visuals? to write the script? Decide on the date that you would like to have the AV finished and work backward.

Secure signed photo release forms (samples available from your council) from every person who will appear in your AV. Remember that a parent or guardian must sign for a minor.

4. *The audio.* Develop an audio track for your AV. It may be all music, a script that will be read by a narrator, testimonials that will be recorded live during the shooting, or a combination of techniques. The timing of the total audio track is very important, as it must exactly match the length of the visual. If your audio will be a combination of several techniques, time each element separately and allow one-second leeway on each piece. You will need these extra seconds when the complete track is edited together.

5. *The storyboard.* Develop a storyboard for your audiovisual. Match appropriate visuals to the audio you created in the previous activity. Remember that the timing of the audio and the video in each scene must match exactly. You will use this storyboard as a guide for shooting the visual portion of your AV.

Depending on production needs, it's sometimes more effective to use existing visuals, rather than shooting new ones. A videotape about local history, for instance, might be greatly enhanced by still photographs from an area historical society. An AV that is intended to illustrate Girl Scout membership statistics might make use of computer graphics, another type of visual.

6. *Locations and casting.* Conduct a casting session to fill parts in your audiovisual. A local theater group might help by providing guidelines. When casting for a Girl Scout AV, it's important to represent all segments of the membership, including girls and adults from various geographic areas of your council and people of various racial/ethnic groups. Try to include a variety of Girl Scout age levels, too. Consider the requirements of each part. If lines are to be spoken, for instance, the person you cast must be articulate and confident.

Then, find locations for your AV. Consider what the requirements of each scene are and try to select one or two locations that will work for all scenes. Too many locations complicate your production and extend shooting time. You may need to modify the storyboard if a proper location is unavailable for a given scene. Consider technical requirements. If the location is indoors, is there enough light? If outdoors, where in the sky will the sun be at shooting time? Consider also the needs of your cast and crew. Are rest rooms nearby? Are dressing rooms necessary?

7. *Production.* Using the storyboard you developed earlier, shoot the visuals and record the audio for your AV.

When shooting on location, the director has total control of what takes place when. It's important for one person to be in charge of the production so that things are finished in a consistent and timely manner. Before shooting begins, check the location to see that all necessary equipment and props are there, that the cast is present and ready to go on, that the lighting is as expected, and that all other elements necessary to the shooting are in order.

If audio is to be recorded on location, decide well in advance how this will be accomplished. There are a variety of ways to record audio in the field, including using the built-in microphone in a video camera or using a separate audio recorder. If this is your first AV production, it will be much simpler to record your audio in a studio, where sound effects and music can be edited in as needed. Most radio stations have good studios and, depending on station policy, may provide studio time to Girl Scouts free of charge.

During shooting, you may choose to modify the storyboard in order to avoid a problem or capitalize on an opportunity. If a Daisy Girl Scout offers an adorable ad-lib, for example, you may elect to use this footage instead of the scene that was originally planned.

8. *Postproduction.* Review all the footage or slides shot for your AV and decide which scenes to use. Some shots, for example, may be technically superior to others or a cast member may excel in one scene and do poorly in another. Pick the very best scenes for your AV and time each one, remembering that the length of every scene must match the length of the audio segment that accompanies it. List all the scenes and their respective audio segments on paper. For videotape and audiotape, note where the selected segment is by using the counter numbers on the recorder. This list is called a "paper edit" and it is used as a guide when supervising the final edit of the AV.

Your final edit will take different forms, depending on which media you elected to use for your AV. If you are using color slides with a live script, then you must type the script clean and indicate at which points the projector operator needs to change slides for the script reader.

If you are using slides with recorded audio, it will probably be simplest to record the final audio track on cassette. There are machines called slide synch recorders that will put an electronic pulse on the cassette each time a new slide should appear on the screen. Then, the cassette may be played on special projection equipment that will automatically advance the slides according to the preset pulses. Check local school districts, college AV departments, or your Girl Scout council to see if this equipment is available to you.

If you are using film or videotape, you will probably need a professional editor to edit your visuals and sound together. Check with the AV departments of local colleges, TV stations, advertising agencies, or film and video production facilities to see about final editing options. Some individuals, however, now own sophisticated home video editing equipment and may volunteer to assist you.

Whatever method is used, you will want to supervise the final editing of your AV. This means being present when the editing is done and discussing your needs with the editor. A good film or videotape editor can very often enhance your production by contributing creative ideas and suggestions during the edit session, so think of that individual as an important part of your production team.

9. *Evaluation.* Screen your AV for a group of people who had no part in its production and ask them to critique it for you. Does your message come through? How does the AV look on screen? Is the technical quality acceptable? What did the audience like best? least?

Screen the AV yourself. Does it say or do what you intended? Did you bring it in on budget? on time? What will you do differently in your next production?

Auto Maintenance

Have you been counting the days until you get your learner's permit to drive a car? Or are you already a licensed driver, seeing the world from behind a steering wheel? Whether you drive now or plan to drive in the future, one thing is certain — driving is not as easy or trouble-free as it seems. Cars are complex machines with thousands of parts, all of which have to work together. Understanding how a car works and maintaining it in good working order are two signs of a responsible driver. So, if there's an automobile in your future, why not develop your knowledge and skills in auto maintenance now.

Complete eight activities, including the five that are starred.

1. Find out what the procedures are in your state for obtaining a learner's permit and a license to drive a car and for registering, insuring, financing, and purchasing a car. Find out how taking driver's education courses at your school can influence requirements to drive and insure a car.

2. Find out what all the controls, switches, indicator lights, gauges, and warning buzzers in a car are for and how to use or respond to them.

3. Go comparison shopping. Compare the cost, resale value, convenience, and safety of two motor vehicles, such as one new and one used; or one compact and one luxury; or one foreign and one American; or a passenger car and pick-up truck. Choose the vehicles through a newspaper or with the help of an automobile dealer.

*4. Plan and/or assemble an auto emergency tool kit. Include items such as the following: a flashlight, flares, reflectors; hand tools such as pliers and a screwdriver; spare parts such as a fan belt and fuses; and a first-aid kit. Show how to use each item safely.

   Demonstrate that you know how to act in each of these highway emergencies: flat tire, car breakdown, accident, car out of gas.

*5. Make a ready reference list of these specifications for use with a particular vehicle:

   • number of quarts of engine oil needed and recommended type and weight of oil for each season

   • oil filter brand and model number

   • air filter brand and model number

   • spark plug brand, number, and size

   • fuse sizes (amps)

   • tire size and pressure

   • type of automatic transmission fluid

   • type of power steering fluid

   • type of brake fluid.

*6. After learning the appropriate safety techniques, and with your consultant's approval, demonstrate your knowledge and skills in the following areas:

   Cooling system inspection: Inspect the radiator and hoses for leakage. Check the coolant level in the system. Know the type of coolant used and when it should be changed. Know what to do if the radiator overheats.

   Battery care: Check the water level on unsealed types of batteries and know how and when to fill them and to what level. Clean battery terminals and the case. Under supervision, learn how to use jumper cables safely to start a car when the battery is dead.

   Tire care: Check the tire pressure with a gauge; put air into the tires; change a tire under supervision; know why tires are rotated and how this is done. Recognize signs and causes of uneven wear. Learn about the different types of tires: glass and steel-belted radial tires, regular tires, studded and plain snow tires.

Fuel: Pump gasoline; know the various types of automotive fuel and their uses.

Fuses: Determine the size and amperage of different fuses in a car. Change a fuse; know how a fuse operates.

Lights: Change a headlight, tail light, and dashboard bulb. Know how to tell a bulb's size, strength, and type of base.

Spark plugs: Remove, gap, and install a spark plug; know how to tell if a spark plug is loose or if a spark plug wire is damaged.

*7. Check the engine oil, automatic transmission fluid, brake fluid, and power steering fluid in several vehicles. Refer to your "spec" sheet and list how much the vehicles need of each type and what to do if the level of any of the fluids is down.

*8. Find out how often the following procedures should be done on a vehicle and obtain some cost estimates for each:

  • oil change; automatic transmission fluid change

  • reline brakes

  • realign wheels and balance tires

  • replace belts, steering lines, and hoses

  • replace damaged or loose parts in exhaust system

  • replace shock absorbers.

9. Change the oil and oil filter on a vehicle. Find an ecologically sound way of getting rid of the old oil. Find out how to recycle oil in your community.

10. Either observe or assist someone doing a complete tune-up on an engine. Figure out the cost of the parts used.

11. Compute the cost of running a car for a year. Include the cost of gasoline, insurance, registration, parking, taxes, and maintenance. Compare this with the cost of using public transportation. Is the convenience of a car worth the expense?

12. Participate in or conduct your own automobile safety workshop. Select a location for this activity, such as a shopping mall, parking lot, county fair, or school. Plan how to attract people who will be interested in learning about basic automotive care. Emphasize safety through preventive maintenance. For example, you might inspect treads on tires or determine whether electrical parts like lights and wipers are in good working order.

Career Exploration

Are you beginning to wonder what you'll be doing a few years from now? Do you find yourself reading all about those new careers suddenly emerging for women? If so, then you're probably ready to do some career exploration of your own.

Choosing a career nowadays is almost like choosing a new sweater — there are so many choices, you hardly know what to select. Deciding about a career, however, is not as simple as all that. First you must look at yourself, your skills, and your interests, tying these into the available career opportunities. Then comes the task of learning about the job market. Gradually you are making decisions that will point the way toward real career satisfaction for you. Career Exploration will help you do every one of these things.

Complete seven activities, including the three that are starred.

*1. Invite a person from an employment agency, a high school or college career counselor, a representative from a women's counseling organization, or a person responsible for hiring staff for an organization or business, to speak to your group. Ask this person about job opportunities for teenagers in your community, effective job search techniques, interviewing do's and don'ts, ways to prepare for careers that interest you, and what you can expect during the first year in the career you are now considering. What are the requirements, responsibilities, salaries, frustrations, and fulfillments of that work? Ask for suggestions on how what you already know and can do could be used in a variety of careers.

*2. Interview at least two people, preferably women, who have careers that you are considering. Learn about their careers and lifestyles. Decide on a way to record and share what you have learned about each person. You might write a career newsletter, develop a slide/tape show or movie, or make up posters or career cards like those in *From Dreams to Reality: Career Cards.*

3. Take a career interest inventory to determine your career interests. Many schools offer tests like this, and perhaps your school guidance counselor could help you locate one to take. Your Girl Scout council may be able to help you find one, too. Based upon the results of the inventory, identify at least three career possibilities you might explore further.

*4. Fill out a job application form for an actual job or one you would like to have. You might obtain a blank form from a business or service organization, explaining why you need it. Have a consultant such as a placement counselor help you prepare your application, checking it for clarity, completeness, neatness, and persuasive ability.

5. Pick a job that has traditionally been held by members of one sex. (For example: Nurses have traditionally been female; bankers have traditionally been male.) Interview a woman and a man who both have the job you chose. Ask them their feelings about their job, including whether they feel their sex was an asset or a limitation in finding, performing, or advancing in it.

OR

Interview at least three women who have different career lifestyles. You might speak to:

• a single businesswoman

• a woman who has changed jobs frequently by choice, because of family relocation owing to her husband's employment, or because of loss of job

• a woman who works in a family-owned business or in a joint professional relationship

• a woman either married, separated, divorced, or widowed who has one or more children

• a woman who has made a change from a volunteer to a paid job, using skills and interests she developed as a volunteer.

Plan and execute a way to share what you learn with others — a discussion, a visual presentation, a story, a picture essay, a panel discussion, or a council-sponsored Girl Scout event.

6. Arrange to spend at least three hours with a person whose career you are considering. During this time, learn about and practice what you would do in this career. Share what you have learned about yourself and this career with friends or family.

7. Attend a career fair or career day arranged by your school, religious organization, community, or Girl Scout council.

OR

Visit a business or industry, large or small, and speak to at least three of the following:

- a person who supervises at least three people

- a person who hires people for the company

- a person who writes, types, or files reports

- a person whose job involves making the products the company sells or delivering the services the organization offers

- a person who handles money or financial information.

Ask them about the nature of their job, what is expected of them on their job, the satisfying and dissatisfying aspects of their work, preparation requirements for their job, opportunities for advancement, and job conditions.

8. Identify at least three jobs listed in your local newspaper, or through your school or community job placement office or library, that you would be interested in applying for, either now or in the future. Write a letter of application and a résumé geared to one of your choices. (See the chapter "From Dreams to Reality: Career Exploration" in the *Cadette and Senior Girl Scout Handbook* for tips on résumé writing.) Have a group partner or consultant look over your letter and résumé and make suggestions for its improvement.

OR

Set up a system to share job opportunities for youth with interested teenagers. You might run a council-sponsored service, produce a newsletter, or publicize jobs on a bulletin board. Plan a way to work through your school, religious organization, or in cooperation with other youth agencies in your community. Make and keep ongoing contacts with local businesses, organizations, and industries so that you will be the first to know about available jobs. Business organizations such as a local chamber of commerce or business clubs might be able to help you.

9. Get a volunteer or salaried job. Keep a diary of each workday. At the end of your workday, recall and record your experiences and impressions. Keep the diary for at least 10 hours of accumulated work time.

10. Write to at least two organizations for information regarding careers you are considering.

11. Talk with at least one person who is knowledgeable about career training opportunities. You might ask your school counselor, a representative of an industry or business, a spokesperson of a college, training institute, vocational school, or a person involved in on-the-job career and apprenticeship training programs.

Computers

Computers touch many areas of our lives. They control toys and help run some factories. Computers keep track of individual savings accounts as well as the finances of multinational corporations. Computers are a source of entertainment; for example, electronic games on home computer screens are a challenge and a delight. Computers also help organize our lives and make them easier. High-speed, sophisticated computers keep government and industry running smoothly by storing and processing countless bits of information. To learn more about these fascinating machines and what they can do, try this interest project.

Complete eight activities.

1. Find out about the four generations of computers. How did the first computer, Univac, differ from the microcomputers and minicomputers of today? Find out what mainframe computers do. Share your findings with a group.

2. Women have always been in the forefront of the computer industry. Find out about the contributions of women in the development of computers. Prepare a presentation for younger children about the achievements of women in computer science.

3. Computer systems are made up of five components: hardware, software, data, procedures, and, of course, the users. *Hardware* is the actual machine; *software* contain the programs that tell the computer what to do; *data* is the information the computer will process; *procedures* give instructions on how to use the computer; *users* are the people who operate the computer. Look through catalogs or visit stores to find out what hardware and software are available and design a system of these components that could help with your schoolwork or some other responsibility.

4. To develop a computer program, you need to be able to divide any activity into a series of logical, sequential steps. One way to write computer program logic is through a flowchart. A flowchart uses symbols to show each step in an activity. For an example of a flowchart, see page 151 in the *Junior Girl Scout Handbook.* Make a flowchart of a complex activity like planning a trip to resident camp or earning the Girl Scout Gold Award.

5. Find out about and compile a directory of job opportunities in the computer industry. Be sure to include information about the training required for each position and the places where you might obtain training in your area.

6. Although computers can complete complex mathematical tasks very quickly, they cannot reason nor do they have emotions or feelings. Participate in a debate about whether computers should be developed to run government offices. What would be the advantages and disadvantages?

7. Find out about the ways computers are used in your community. How are they used in hospitals, in law enforcement, and in government? Find a way to inform others about the use of computers in your community.

8. Write a short story that projects how computers are part of your community in the year 2020.

9. Find out about computer graphics. What kinds of images can be generated by a computer? Monitor the graphics in three computer games. What are the images used? How lifelike are they? How is movement portrayed? How do the images increase the appeal of the games?

OR

If you have access to a computer, develop your own computer graphics.

10. Computer systems range in price from relatively inexpensive to systems costing millions. Visit stores and look through catalogs to find current prices of home and small-business computers. Determine what you would need if you were to put together a home computer system for your family that cost $500. $3,000? Be sure to include software as well as hardware. Compare the speed, memory size, and program execution capabilities of the two systems.

11. Find out if computers are used in your school or Girl Scout council. If they are, what functions are the computers performing? What results are being achieved? Find out why the decision was made to computerize or not to computerize. Share your findings with others.

12. Write your own computer-related activity that takes advantage of computer resources available to you.

Energy Awareness

Oil rigs in the ocean, windmills in the countryside, bike paths in the city? These are but a few of today's solutions to tomorrow's energy problems. The unhappy fact is that the world's known supply of natural resources is slowly diminishing. At the same time, the consumption of oil and gas continues to increase more rapidly than ever. Though many people all over the globe are working to find solutions to energy problems, there are still many unanswered questions.

Becoming aware of how energy affects your own life and what you can do to help conserve energy, even on a small scale, is what this interest project is all about. You may find the subject so fascinating that you'll list energy research as a career to consider.

Complete eight activities, including the two that are starred.

*1. Arrange to visit your local electric utility company or one of its power plants, or have someone from the utility company speak to your group. Find out how electricity is produced in your area and what causes brownouts and blackouts. Ask about some of the problems facing the utility companies today and their concerns about supplying energy for the future. Find out if your utility company is using nuclear or solar power or other alternative energy sources and, if so, why it has chosen to do so. Think of other questions to ask about energy and nuclear and solar power for today and tomorrow.

2. Find out how much it costs to operate the electric appliances in your kitchen or another room in your house for a week.

   Identify the high-energy appliances and think of ways to reduce their use. This is how to do it:

   (a) Find the wattage of the appliance. This should appear on a label on the appliance.

   (b) Multiply the wattage by the estimated hours of use in a week's time and divide by 1,000 to obtain the number of kilowatt-hours (kwh).

   (c) Multiply the number of kwh's by the local electrical rate, which you can get from your utility company. Add taxes and you have the approximate cost of using the appliance per week.

   OR

   Learn how to read a home electric meter. A representative from your electric company might show you how to do this. Keep a record of the number of kilowatt-hours of electricity your family uses in one week. For the following week, work out a plan with your family to make a conscious effort to cut down on the use of electricity. Check the meter at the end of the second week. Was there a noticeable difference? If so, are there ways to continue the savings? Share with your troop or group some ways your family saved on energy.

*3. Make plans for the possibility that your dwelling might be without electricity for three to five days. How will you keep warm or cool, cook food and keep it fresh, keep water pipes from freezing, and do your homework? Prepare a set of plans to carry your family through such an experience. Include plans for cooperation between neighbors to make the situation better for everyone.

4. Make an energy survey of your home or, as a troop or group activity, make a survey of your meeting place. (To do an energy survey, you must check the whole house or building for possible sources of heat or cooling loss, such as poorly fitting doors, and inefficient uses of energy in the building.) Make suggestions to remedy the energy waste. Carry out at least one of your suggestions.

   OR

   Make an energy survey of an automobile. Does it use gas economically or not? Has the engine been tuned recently? Do the tires have the proper inflation? Are the air and oil filters clean? Talk to a car owner or mechanic about energy conservation in the use and maintenance of cars. Find out about driving habits that save gas. Try to do something about improving the car's energy efficiency.

OR

Find out what a heat pump is, how it works, its cost, where it is used, and its advantages compared to other ways of heating or cooling. Try to see one in operation.

OR

Investigate the pros and cons of using coal or wood stoves as a source of heat and using alternate energy sources, such as wind and water power and solar energy.

5. Suppose there is a severe oil (petroleum) shortage and the government requires you and your community to cut back on the use of oil to conserve the available supply. Prepare a plan to help your family and community respond to this emergency. Begin by finding out which of the products you use are made from oil. (Plastics and heating oil are two examples.) Next, find out which of the services you use are oil-dependent. (Examples of those providing services are utility companies and hospitals.) Then decide how your family and community can cut back on oil use, and how the community can provide people with necessary products and services. Find out if your community has emergency plans to cope with an oil shortage. If not, share your ideas with a local government official.

6. Visit a recycling center and find out when and how recycling can save energy. Carry out a recycling project or volunteer your services at a recycling center.

OR

Make recycled paper out of newspaper or other discarded paper. Find out how it is done commercially.

7. Do at least one of the following:

   • Build a solar cooker and cook part of a meal on it.

   • Make a simple solar still for getting drinkable water.

   • Build a model solar water heater that works and demonstrate its use to someone who has never seen one or to your council's camp director or committee.

   • Build your own solar energy project or other type of energy project.

8. Go to a building supply store and ask to see examples of insulating materials. Find out the meaning of the term "R-values" and what the recommended R-values are for ceilings, outside walls, and floors in your area.

Try to find out what type of insulation is used in your home or school within the frame (walls, floors, and ceilings). Look at the way windows and doors are insulated and how plants and trees are used to keep out drafts and cut the force of the wind. Find out whether your home needs additional insulation to improve energy efficiency. If possible, watch insulation being installed or help to insulate a house, apartment, or building.

9. Radiation is all around and is part of the natural as well as the human-made environment. By filling out this form, compute your radiation dose to get an idea of the average amount of radiation you are exposed to every year. People who work with radioactive materials are allowed 5,000 units per year without harmful effects.

	Your Annual Total
Location: Cosmic radiation that reaches the earth	44 units
Elevation: Add 1 unit for every 100 feet (31 meters) your town is located above sea level. (Coastal cities are at sea level, so add zero.)	_____

If your house is: brick   add 45 units
              stone   add 50 units
              wood   add 35 units
              concrete add 45 units
	_____

Ground radiation (U.S. average)	15 units
Water, food, air radiation (U.S. average)	25 units
Nuclear weapons-testing fallout	4 units
If you've had a chest X ray, add nine units for each one you had this year.	_____
If you've had a series of intestinal X rays, add 210 units for each series you had this year.	_____
If you've flown in a jet airplane during the year, add one unit for each 1,500 miles (2,400 km) you have traveled.	_____
If you watch color television, add 0.15 units for each of the hours you watch in an average day.	_____
If you live near a nuclear power plant, add the following for each hour you are home in an average day:	
If you live one mile away, add 0.02 units per hour per day.	_____
If you live more than one but less than five miles away, add 0.0002 units per hour per day.	_____
If you live more than five miles away, add zero.	_____
TOTAL	_____

10. Choose an energy source for today or tomorrow and become an "expert" on it. Find out its advantages and disadvantages, the reserves available, governmental controls and restrictions on it, its environmental impact, and the prospects of its meeting mass energy needs. Prepare a short energy commercial for radio or television to sell your energy source to the public. Try it out on an audience. You might check with your local radio or television station to see if it would use your commercial.

11. Put on a series of skits for an outside audience showing the importance of conserving energy resources. Show how fuel shortages can contribute to unemployment and business failure. Show ways that people can ease the situation. Find out from your audience what they can do to use energy resources wisely. Try to have a local government official present to tell what local, state, and federal government agencies are doing to conserve resources.

OR

Put on a puppet show or other kind of show for younger children in a school, a hospital, or a Girl Scout troop or group about ways they can help to conserve energy. Make it fun and informative.

Entrepreneurship

An entrepreneur is a person who starts her or his own business. An entrepreneur recognizes a need, and puts creativity and ingenuity with action to provide an innovative service or product just right for the customer. Such a person is willing to take risks because of the vision of success and profit. This interest project will help you find out if you have the temperament, skills, and ability to become an entrepreneur.

Complete eight activities, including the three that are starred.

1. Prepare an exhibit of resources on entrepreneurship, including book reviews and articles from magazines and financial journals. Share this exhibit with others.

2. Investigate the lives and experiences of a few contemporary entrepreneurs; be sure that they represent a diversity of people. Write an article, or create a collage or poster, exhibiting the differences and similarities in their personalities, experiences, and achievements.

3. In our fast-paced world, change is rapid and constant. New products and services are introduced almost daily. Many fail, others succeed and then fade, and some may even dramatically change our lives. List three innovations developed in the last five years that have significantly affected your life. Decide how these innovations have improved the quality of your life or your work, and what specific needs they have fulfilled.

   Share your findings in a presentation discussion with your Girl Scout troop or group.

*4. Do a self-assessment of your own interests, strengths, and talents.

   Identify a group of people — your target market — with needs that match your interests, and explore fully what kinds of products or services would better serve their needs.

   Keeping in mind your own strengths and abilities, determine a product or service that you could provide to meet the needs of your target market.

*5. Focus groups are often used to increase the potential success of a new product or service. Using an idea you have for an innovative product or service, interview people who would be potential users or customers. Ask questions to test your idea. Pay attention to their answers and also to questions they ask of you. What improvements or modifications of your idea can you make, based on your findings?

*6. Write up a proposal describing in full detail your product or service.

   • Identify the potential customers who might use it.

   • Describe how the product/service compares with the competition.

   • Describe how you would distribute your product or service: for example, direct mail, door-to-door, in stores.

7. Research advertising media, including TV, radio, and print. Create an advertisement for a product or service. Share your advertisement with people who might be future consumers. Ask for their responses to the ad.

8. Write to several agencies or institutions that support entrepreneurship. Find out about the services they offer, fees for membership, etc. Don't forget about federal and state agencies that support small-business owners and consumers.

9. The greatest problem facing women entrepreneurs is the start-up funding needed to get their projects underway. To explore possible funding, talk to bankers, venture capitalists, and other lending institutions to see what they require of potential borrowers. Keep a log and compare the various requirements.

10. Research grants available to entrepreneurs and write for information regarding proposal requirements, types of businesses previously funded, the number of women who have applied for and have received grants, and the reasons for being accepted or rejected.

11. Partnerships can present both opportunities and problems. Find out what are the advantages and disadvantages of going into business with a partner. What are some of the critical factors to consider? Interview a few entrepreneurs who are presently in partnership with someone else and those who have been but are no longer in partnership.

12. You have a great idea and you want to protect it legally. Find out about the differences between a patent, a trademark, and a copyright. Invite an attorney or someone knowledgeable about business ventures to talk to your Girl Scout troop or group about the legal aspects of starting a new business.

Geology

Are you curious about the history, origin, and structure of the planet that is your home? The earth's crust is just the thinnest shell covering massive layers of increasingly hot and molten materials. Explore the structure of the earth and the dynamic forces that are constantly forming and shaping the planet.

Complete eight activities, including the one that is starred.

1. Make a collection of 20-25 specimens of rocks, minerals, and fossils in any combination. Learn to observe proper safety precautions while collecting specimens. Before entering any private land, get permission from the landowner. The best sources for collecting are excavations in bedrock, road cuts in solid rock, and cuts made by streams. Be able to tell about the mineral composition of at least five specimens and how each was formed. Accurately identify and label each specimen.

2. Collect several types of soil in your area. Create a soil profile. Determine the types of soil in your collection. Show how the soil horizons vary in different areas. Separate a soil sample into its components and describe each. Be careful not to miss the ones that are invisible. Describe the components of soil that are used by plants.

3. What are the sources of all the energy your family uses — coal, fuel oil, hydroelectric power? Find out about one energy source — its origin, how it is formed, from where and how it reaches you.

4. There are types of maps that provide varied information about the earth's surface. Topographical maps, geologic plats, and even highway maps can all provide information about the land features of an area. Study several maps of an area in your state and become familiar with the information on the maps. Make a sketch map that highlights the interesting facts you found.

*5. Go on a day hike in an area with some interesting geological features. Examine interesting structures and formations, streams, erosion, fossils, etc. Make sketches or take photographs of the major features of the area you've hiked. As you are hiking, discuss with your hiking companions how the original inhabitants of that area probably made use of the local geological features.

6. Find out the courses of earthquakes and the frequency with which they occur in your state. Learn about faults and plate tectonics. If possible, visit a facility where earthquakes are monitored, or find out how a seismograph works. Learn the safety precautions to take during an earthquake.

OR

Find out about volcanoes. Where are the sites of active volcanoes around the world? Learn about lava and the types of minerals and rocks formed from volcanoes and lava flows. How have ancient volcanic eruptions preserved a fossil and archaeological record of the past? Do a brief presentation on one aspect of volcanoes and volcanic eruptions that interests you.

7. Visit places in your area where you can observe the effects of weathering. Possibilities include cemeteries, old store buildings, and areas with severe soil erosion. Find out how weathering occurs and what effect it has on rocks and soils. What effects do heat, freezing temperatures, wind, plants, water, and acid rain have on weathering processes?

8. Grow your own crystals. Describe or photograph the process of crystal formation. What products do we use daily that are crystals? Under what conditions do crystals form in nature?

OR

Find out major minerals which make up planet Earth. Scientists are continually finding out new information about the other planets in our solar system. Compare what we know about Earth's composition with what we now know about the other planets in the solar system. How are their surfaces and atmospheres different from that on Earth?

9. Draw or photograph the coastal features caused by erosion or deposition. Be able to describe what is happening in each picture.

OR

Draw or photograph the features of a river or lake that indicate the presence of erosion or deposition. Be able to describe what is happening in each.

OR

Draw or photograph the landscape features created by glaciation and be able to describe what happened in each picture.

10. Geology and related sciences offer a wide variety of careers to explore, including fields such as engineering, geophysics, petrology, hydrology, geochemistry, paleontology, planetary geology, and oceanographic geology. Select an area of earth science that fascinates you and interview someone who has made a career in that field. If possible, spend a day with that person to learn more about her or his area of interest.

11. Do a project to reduce erosion in your area. Devise a method to show that your project has halted or reduced erosion. The project might include planting trees, shrubs, or dune grasses. You might reduce trail erosion at a natural area or campsite by relocating the trail to avoid steep grades or wet areas, or adding steps and barriers in appropriate places.

12. Find out about different types of fossils, including how they are formed and the clues they give us about the history of the earth and the life it has supported. Try to observe actual fossil samples. Make a fossil map of your area, showing the life forms that left their trace in the earth's crust.

High-Tech Communication

We relate to each other in a high-tech world. Messages are beamed by microwaves to orbiting satellites; fiber optics instantaneously transmit voices from coast to coast; and computers are revolutionizing everything from printing to TV communications. Yesterday's science fiction gadgets are today's real technological equipment. You are already a high-tech communicator! Every time you dial a phone or turn on the TV, you become part of a vast communications network. Explore the many facets of being a modern communicator in the following activities.

Complete eight activities.

1. Visit a computer store or center or consult a catalog to learn about home computers. Then decide which of your needs and/or those of your family (bookkeeping, recreation, chore monitoring, school tasks, etc.) could be handled by a home computer. Explore what kind of setup you would need. Find out about the different types of components (hardware and software) that are available. Compare costs and add-on capabilities. Keep a record of your findings for possible future reference.

OR

Find out how many kinds of different tasks home computers can be programmed to do. Determine whether programs can be purchased for these tasks or whether you can program the tasks yourself. Share your list so you can help others know what kind of computer "helps" are available.

2. *RAM, ROM, PROM, bit, byte, chip, disk, data, digital* are not the words to a nonsense poem, but just some of the key words used when working with computers. In addition, there are several computer languages, such as BASIC, COBOL, and FORTRAN, that are used when "talking" to computers. Compile a list of computer terms and their meanings so you will be literate in the language of computers. Include the terms that introduce this activity. Compare your list with another and decide which terms are most important to know, or use a computer terminal to demonstrate that you understand your terms.

3. Make a videotape. Many school systems and groups have videotape equipment that you might be able to use, or you may have access to a home VCR (videocassette recorder) and video camera. For whatever equipment you use, learn the factors that can improve or lessen the quality of your final tape.

OR

Visit a video equipment store and see a videodisc and videocassette-recorder demonstration. Learn the advantages and disadvantages of each system. Compare considerations such as cost, durability, and adaptability. Determine which system you would buy if you had the opportunity. Write a brief "consumer critique" or advertisement based on your findings.

4. Many areas are now served by cable TV companies. Contact your local cable TV distributor to find out what kind of public access is available. Many companies offer courses and/or the opportunity to become involved in original community programming. Take advantage of what they offer, or arrange to take a tour of their "originating station" to view the equipment and the operation.

5. Learn how to hook up an audio system of a type that could be used in a home or school. This system should have at least three different components. For most systems, the basics would be a receiver, a turntable, and speakers. Find out what other components the system can take: for example, a tape deck, auxiliary speakers, preamplifiers. Make certain you understand terms such as *Dolby, input, output, ground, monophonic, stereophonic, quadraphonic.* Comparison-shop so you can compare the value of the various brands of components.

6. Make an audiotape. There are many types of systems and methods used in audio recording — for example, tape-to-tape, record-to-tape, or live taping using microphones. Try to involve your troop or group. You might even coordinate your recording with a slide show for a group presentation. When you produce your tape, whether you use cassette or reel-to-reel, know what factors will affect your recording. Make sample recordings so you can hear some of the things that can offset your recording — input levels that are too high or low, incorrect setting for the type of tape used, use of Dolby, having the microphone too close to or too far from the source, etc.

7. Assemble a piece of communication equipment. Many types of equipment, ranging from simple radios and phone equipment to home computers and video sets, are available in kits ready for assembly. You might even design your own piece of equipment, using a variety of improvised components. Demonstrate your equipment design and function to an interested group or person. Be sure to explain the basic parts and describe how the equipment operates.

8. Learn about types of equipment that are designed to help people with disabilities communicate — special telephones, closed-caption TV programming for the hearing-impaired, and electronic Braille scanners, for example. Some devices are designed to help provide access to regular equipment, while others enhance the senses. Make a list of your findings. Find out how you can help people with disabilities. (You could contact local hospitals or schools that have programs of this type.) This could be a good service project for you to become involved in.

9. Explore long-range communication. We have moved from local to transcontinental to worldwide communication, and now can beam messages to the moon and beyond. We truly have become a global community.

   Listen to a radio that has at least five different reception bands (AM and FM are generally standard). Keep a record of the farthest distance, the different countries of origin, and the types of broadcasts you were able to monitor on each band.

OR

Find out about the new technologies, such as fiber optics, lasers, and satellites, that are improving telephone communication, especially transcontinental calls. Arrange a visit to a telephone company station to see some of this technology in action. Find out how new technical capabilities affect your total phone service. Share your findings with your troop or group.

10. Learn how to operate at least three of the following:

    Telecopier

    shortwave radio (CB or ham)

    telepage (message beeper)

    automatic banking machine

    cordless telephone

    film projector

    slide projector

    word processor

    loudspeaker system

    videodisc or compact-disc player

    intercom system.

OR

Play at least three different computer games or, if you have access to a personal computer, create your own game. Show the strategy of one prepackaged game or your own game by preparing a simple flowchart. This should outline the step-by-step alternatives that are possible when playing the game.

11. Survey your community to find out what types of communication tools and technological equipment are used in emergency situations. Include hospitals, ambulance services, and police and fire departments in your search. Whenever possible, make arrangements to see the emergency resources list based upon your findings. While doing your survey, note community needs; you might find some good ideas for a community service project.

12. Communications technology is a vast field. Take advantage of an opportunity unique to your area and develop your own activity. Some ideas to consider are touring a local radio, TV, or satellite receiving station; working with a ham radio operation for a month or more; helping develop a public service announcement to publicize Girl Scouting; helping construct an individual earth station; making a slide/tape presentation; and/or investigating local businesses (real estate offices, banks, department stores), organizations, or public services that rely on modern communications technology.

OR

Interview two different people who work in some aspect of communications. (You might follow the format of *From Dreams to Reality: Career Cards*.) Be sure to find out about the educational training required for their jobs and the current salary ranges; ask them whether their particular jobs have changed in the past few years (or did not even exist a few years ago) and/or whether they anticipate great changes in the future.

Money Management

Money — it's nice to have, pleasurable to spend, and hard to hold on to. For some people, money management becomes an exciting career; for others, money remains a daily challenge. Knowing how to stretch your dollars from allowance to allowance, or from payday to payday, requires planning and attention to details. But, it really can be done!

No matter how little or how much money you have, you can learn the skills of money management and apply them to your earnings and spending habits. The reward? You'll soon find that your dollars make sense.

Complete eight activities.

1. Visit places where you can save money and obtain a checking account — perhaps a savings or commercial bank, a savings and loan association, or a credit union. Or talk to someone from any one of these organizations who specializes in savings and checking.

   To learn about policies in savings, collect information on different types of savings accounts, including certificates of deposit. With your group, compare rates for various types of savings accounts. Become familiar with deposit and withdrawal forms, passbooks, and laws governing savings accounts.

   Explore checking by determining the various types of checking accounts offered by different banks and some credit unions. Select a particular kind of checking account and find out how to:

   - open an account
   - write a check
   - keep an ongoing record of credits and debits
   - reconcile a bank statement
   - avoid overdrafts
   - report errors
   - compute and compare fees charged for different services
   - use the special privileges granted, if any.

   Also, learn about the uses of safety deposit boxes and travelers' checks and how to obtain them.

2. Arrange to go along on a field trip with a local real estate broker or rental agent. Become familiar with terms commonly used in real-estate transactions. Discuss the pros and cons of several properties currently on the market. Learn the basic types of mortgages and leases and their advantages and disadvantages.

3. Prepare a monthly budget for a family. Determine the total income and size of the family before you work on the budget.

   OR

   Prepare an ideal budget for yourself for a specified period of time, indicating money you get (from family and jobs you do) and where it goes. Try to stay on your ideal budget for a period of time. Does this ideal budget resemble how you actually manage money? What would you want to change about your spending, earning, and saving patterns?

4. How would you find a part-time, summer, or full-time job? How do people in your community find jobs? Visit a state employment office or a personnel agency or have a representative talk with your group. Find out how this organization helps people obtain employment. Learn the steps you would have to take to find a job.

   OR

   Do the activities in the "From Dreams to Reality: Career Exploration" chapter of the *Cadette and Senior Girl Scout Handbook.*

5. Visit an unemployment office, a social security office, or invite a representative from one of these offices to speak to your group. Find out how persons who are unable to work as a result of age, disability, or lack of jobs, receive services or get money or goods through governmental programs. Explore plans offered by employers, unions, or cooperatives that offer benefits for employees or members.

6. Talk to an insurance salesperson at a company, a bank, or an independent agency about the various types of insurance; their cost, the protection they offer, and the advantages and disadvantages of each type. Find out

about types of insurance that cover a person's life, health, home, personal property, and automobile. Prepare a chart that could be used to explain this to others.

7. Under the guidance of an investment counselor, broker, or knowledgeable adult, learn about the workings of the stocks and bonds markets. Find out what mutual funds are. Then do one of the following:

- Talk to a knowledgeable person about the various types of stock — common and preferred and mutual funds, the ways stocks can be purchased, and the pros and cons of each type of investment. Then, with your consultant, discuss how to purchase stocks and shares of mutual funds. Imagine that you have a sum of money to spend on stocks, bonds, and/or mutual funds. With your consultant's help, decide what you would purchase. Follow your purchase(s) in the stock-market page of a newspaper for a certain period of time. Did you make or lose money on your investment? What can you learn about investing for the time when you actually have money to spend?

OR

- Investigate other ways of investing money — property, commodities, artwork, antiques, precious stones, or metals. Become familiar with the pros and cons of each type of investment. Decide which investment would suit you best and follow an imaginary purchase over a period of time.

8. Try computing the income tax you might owe. To do this, you will need federal, state, and, in some cases, city income-tax information booklets and forms. They are available from your local U.S. Government Internal Revenue Service office, and often can be found in post offices, state or city offices, or local banks.

- Prepare an income tax return for the money you are making in a job now and based upon the number of exemptions claimed on the withholding form you filled out for your employer when you began work. You will probably want to use the short form, form 1040A, to figure your federal income tax.

OR

- Determine the income you think you will be making your first year out of school or college and the probable lifestyle you will have. Will you be single or married, have or not have children, rent or own a home, have expenses for education and health, etc.? Prepare an income tax return statement based upon the number of exemptions you will have in this life situation.

9. Keep a record of the food you or your family eats and its cost over a period of time. By reading magazines and brochures and seeking advice from a home economics teacher or nutritionist, discover ways you can cut costs and still maintain high nutritional value in your diet. Explore ways people in this and other countries meet their dietary needs using inexpensive foods. Develop menus for a week based on your findings for cutting costs and try them for at least a week. Compare your new budget costs with your earlier records.

10. Invite a consumer credit counselor or manager to talk to you or your group about how credit can be established to purchase the goods and services your family uses.

You might explore the following topics together:

- the different types of credit and their cost, in dollars and interest charges. Include charge accounts, revolving credit plans, installment or time-payment plans, credit cards, cash loans, and loans made by banks, commercial loan companies, and credit unions.

- the credit application procedures of several firms, such as a department store, gasoline company, or bank

- facts that are considered when a credit application is being decided upon

- the purpose of a credit rating — how it is determined and how it is used

- how to fill out a credit application and how to determine the rights and responsibilities of the purchaser and seller

- ways to remedy the problem of overextended credit.

11. Make a list of countries you would like to visit. Investigate: (1) what money is called in each of these countries and what the rate of exchange on United States currency would be; (2) how, when, and where you might exchange money into the currency of a foreign country as you travel; (3) any other facts concerning money you should know before you travel, such as laws, currency restrictions, and bargaining.

12. Conduct a money management seminar for another Girl Scout troop or group, your parents, or a community group. Choose topics and a discussion level that will interest your group.

You might include these topics:

- for younger teenagers — budgeting, savings, ways to earn money

- for adults — savings, checking, insurance, mortgages, investments, career information, ways to cut household expenses

- for adults 60 and over — include social security, investments, ways to cut household expenses, conserving resources (savings, property), government-supported programs for the elderly.

Include consultants you have worked with in this project. You might plan small group workshops, a panel discussion, or a formal presentation.

OR

Interview one or more people who have careers in money management.

Plant Culture

Plants are the producers of our world. Food, paper, fabrics, medicines, building materials, the touch of life that brightens homes and working environments, even the fuels we burn, come from plants. Explore the plant world through this interest project.

Complete eight activities, including the one that is starred.

1. Do a soil test on a soil sample obtained from an area where you would like to plant something. Good soil is essential for healthy plant growth, and many factors can affect soil quality. Consult a gardening manual or similar resource to find out how to test a soil sample. Many garden supply stores have inexpensive soil-testing kits available. Find out what can be added to soil to improve its quality. If possible, do this activity before doing Activity 2.

*2. Plan and plant a garden that will produce at least three food products. Select a suitable plot of land or, if you are an urban gardener, improvise with tubs and containers. Prepare the soil before planting (see Activity 1 for suggestions) and arrange your garden plot for maximum sunlight. Start your plants from seed or young seedling plants. Follow a garden maintenance schedule that includes watering, fertilizing, weeding, and pest control. When you harvest your crop, prepare and share it with someone else or, if possible, enter your produce at a county fair.

3. Select a plant product that interests you and trace its path from farm to consumer. Investigate handling steps and cost increases that occur on the way to the consumer's home. If your product requires any processing, make certain that you find out what is involved in these steps. As carefully as possible, chart the entire route for a display that can educate others about how a familiar home product reaches them from the farm.

OR

Investigate the variety of careers possible in agriculture. Develop at least two career cards, using *From Dreams to Reality: Career Cards* as a model.

4. Start three new plants without using seeds. You can try the same method on three kinds of plants and/or try three methods on the same or different plants. Most basic gardening manuals will have information to help you. Tubers, runners, "eyes," rhizomes, grafting, layering, and cutting are some of the terms to become familiar with as you investigate how to start your plants.

5. Plan and serve a "total plant" menu for one meal. Vegetables are a good start, but there are also plenty of other food items, such as flour or cereal grains, that are made from plant products. Careful investigation will help you find plant substitutes for animal products. Plant oils, fruit juices, nuts, herb teas, bean spreads, tofu, carrageenan and seaweed, and grain varieties such as bulgur wheat and kasha are just some of the ingredients you should consider. An extra touch could be serving the meal with total plant accessories such as cotton napkins, linen tablecloths, straw mats, wooden bowls, or bamboo chopsticks.

6. Grow a plant hydroponically (without soil). For best results, consult a gardening book or manual that gives a step-by-step outline of what you will have to do for a successful hydroponics project. Some of the materials you will need are a soilless growing medium (such as vermiculite, perlite, or small pebbles), plant food, suitable containers, and an area where your hydroponics setup can get good light. Monitor your plant's growth for two months, carefully checking for adequate food and water.

OR

Grow edible sprouts from at least two kinds of seeds. Find out about the different factors, such as light and water, that will affect the growth and final flavor of your sprouts.

7. Learn about poisonous weeds, wild plants, or common cultivated plants found in the home and garden. Develop a checklist with at least eight common plants that are poisonous. Chart the name of the plant, the poisonous parts (such as berries, stems, leaves, and sap), symptoms of poisoning, and emergency procedures. Make certain your checklist has emergency phone numbers, especially that of the nearest poison control center.

   Conduct a poison plant education session with a group of younger children. Because of their natural curiosity, inexperience, and small size, young children are the most common victims of accidental poisoning.

8. Find out what protected or endangered species of plants are in your area. Then devise and put into action a plan to preserve and protect them. The list of endangered and protected wildlife includes plants as well as animals. Because of the essential ties between plant and animal life, the eventual loss of any plant can mean the loss of home and/or food for any number of animals. Your plan to protect plant life could include the construction of nature trails and protective walkways, conservation planting, or an awareness campaign in your area.

OR

Survey an area that appears to be suffering from soil erosion (the loss of topsoil). Since almost all land plants depend on their rooting in soil for survival, erosion and loss of topsoil can be devastating. List the factors, such as slope or pitch of the land, vulnerability to wind or water damage, physical wear, lack of plant cover, etc., that may be contributing to the loss of soil. If possible, plan a conservation scheme that you can implement on your own or with a group. Seek help and advice from experts or those knowledgeable about soil conservation. Obtain proper permissions and do your best to preserve and/or rehabilitate the area.

9. Learn about insects in your area that play a beneficial role and those that are responsible for either local or widespread damage. Harmful insects account for mil-

lions of dollars in revenue losses and millions of tons of ruined produce. Find out what can be done to control these insects without destroying the helpful ones — and without harming plants, animals, or people. Are there environmentally safe insecticides, biological controls, or environmental factors that can be used to halt the spread of damage? Share your findings or find out if you can help by volunteering your time and effort.

10. Collect recipes for health and beauty products that are made from plants. Many cultures, past and present, have used plant products that rival today's chemicals in effectiveness. Look for skin balms, hair conditioners, first-aid treatments, facials, and insect repellents. Prepare at least three of your recipes for yourself and someone else.

11. Find an outdoor space that would be improved through landscape architecture (the art and science of relating people to their outdoor environment). Think of the area as an "outdoor room." Make a drawing of the location, indicating what kinds of plants and shrubs you would use and where you would position them. Include other landscape elements such as fences, walkways, benches, lights, signs, water fountains, etc. Make certain your design would be accessible to people with disabilities.

OR

Survey several locations in your area and determine what you would consider the positive and negative aspects of each area. Decide what could be done to improve those locations that have negative aspects. Decide which location in your area would win your "best designed and landscaped" award. Be able to explain the reasons for your choice. Share your findings with someone else.

12. Design your own activity related to plants. Do you live on or near a farm, orchard, or nursery or know someone with a special skill or interest in some aspect of horticulture? Tap into the unique resources available to you when designing your activity.

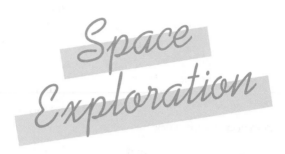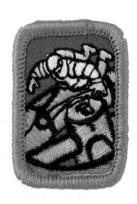

Space Exploration

For centuries, humans have looked to the skies with awe and wonder. Until the second half of this century, imaginations soared but explorations were entirely earthbound. Even with recent technological advances, probings into the nature of the universe are rather limited; the enormous distances of space are still a vastly unexplored frontier. You can be one of the pioneers who ventures into new, unexplored worlds. This interest project will help you begin your discoveries.

Complete seven activities.

1. Modern technology has enabled astronomers to probe ever deeper into the reaches of outer space. Many of the recent discoveries have shown the universe to be filled with far more than the sun, moon, and stars. Find out about at least four of the following astronomical phenomena: *quasars, pulsars, novas, supernovas, black holes, dwarf stars, giant stars, protostars, neutron stars, variable stars, cosmic clouds,* and *globular clusters.* Try to observe the sections of the night sky where these objects are located.

2. Science fiction is a creative look into the future and the possibilities of distant worlds in the universe. Many science-fiction writers use scientific facts as the basis for their fantastic creations. And, in some cases, their fantasies eventually become realities. For example, the idea of humans walking on the moon was once an impossible dream. Read a science-fiction book or short story and decide what elements of the story might be possible and why.

OR

Write your own science-fiction story about life on planet Earth in the future or life elsewhere in the universe.

3. Imagine you are an architect 100 years in the future. Design a human space colony for a planet, a moon, or an asteroid in our solar system. Consider the conditions that will exist on the site that you have selected and include these as considerations in your design.

The design for your colony should include the following:

• purpose of the structure

• living arrangements

• special equipment

• health and safety needs

• environmental protection.

Show your design to someone and explain all the factors that you considered in designing the structure.

4. Visit a museum or other facility that has an exhibit, display, or presentation on aerospace, astronomy, or a related field. Based on your visit, select at least one topic that interested you and explore it further on your own.

5. The skies have always been a source of mystery and curiosity, and humans have attempted to explain the phenomena they saw. Find out about myths, legends, and early theories about the nature of the universe. You might focus on one theme — for example, stories from different cultures that explained the origin of the sun, moon, and stars, or all the different theories about our own star, the sun. Share your findings with others.

6. Build an accurate scale model of a vehicle that is used for space exploration. Find out about its design, function, and basic operation. Be able to help others learn about your vehicle.

OR

Construct something that is capable of flight. Be able to explain the scientific principles on which your "flying object" is based. Determine what actual flight vehicles operate on the same principles.

7. Plan an activity that will help youngsters learn about space and exploration. For example, you might conduct a night-sky exploration for Brownie or Junior Girl

Scouts in a camp setting, build and explain a model of the solar system, put on a play about life on a space station, or tell a story about a woman astronaut, including her training and achievements.

8. Start a career file on jobs related to space exploration. Investigate at least five fields. The chapter "From Dreams to Reality: Career Exploration" in the *Cadette and Senior Girl Scout Handbook* and *From Dreams to Reality: Career Cards* will help you in your work.

9. Develop a booklet or display that highlights women who have played an important role in the history of flight and space exploration.

10. The technologies involved in space exploration are constantly improving. Trace the history of one type of instrument or tool used in space exploration. Compare the early designs of this instrument or tool and the information that scientists were capable of obtaining with the equipment available to them today. Write a forecast of what might be possible by the turn of the century. You might consider investigating spacecraft, telescopes, cameras, or instruments that measure light, infrared and ultraviolet radiation, radio waves, X rays, and other forms of electromagnetic energy.

11. Design your own. Space exploration involves many sciences and disciplines, and the activities in this interest project represent just a small sampling of what you can learn or do. Tap into the unique resources and opportunities available to you and develop your own space exploration activity. Here are some of the things you might do:

- Explore what countries around the world are doing in space exploration.

- Using a telescope, monitor an object in the night sky for a month.

- Visit NASA and, if possible, view the launching of a space vehicle.

- Develop a space exploration resource file. NASA has many educational materials available to the public.

- Keep a scrapbook of news clippings on items related to astronomy and space exploration.

The World of the Arts

Dabbler

Art is all around you. It isn't just the work of an "old master" hanging in a museum. It's something everyone can enjoy and make part of daily living.

Art is the visual arts you appreciate with your eyes: the paintings, drawings, collages, prints, photographs you see in homes, public buildings, books and magazines, and, yes, in museums, too.

Art is sculpture and buildings, the plan of a city, the pottery and furniture you use.

Art is the performing arts of music, dance, drama, and puppetry, which you can see live or appreciate on recordings, film, or television.

Art is everyday practical things — the design on the package you buy, the poster you see, the flower arrangements your florist makes, the colors and patterns in rooms, the way you dress, the way a park is landscaped.

The World of the Arts in Cadette and Senior Girl Scouting can be the introduction to lifelong pursuits. Some people may find they wish to make a career of one form of the arts. But even if you do not pursue art as a career, it can be a hobby or avocation and bring you many hours of lasting joy.

Complete eight activities.

1. "Creativity is the capacity to see new relationships and possibilities in familiar objects or situations." Using this definition, create from your imagination and materials readily available to you a game for others in your troop or group to play. Make up all the rules and parts or equipment for the game. Have a game-sharing session and decide which were the most creative games.

2. Architecture is an art form you live with every day. You work and play, eat and sleep in structures designed by architects. You see works of architecture constantly and they affect your life more than you realize.

   Design and create a model out of Styrofoam, cardboard, or wood that you feel would be a dwelling for a city or farm approximately 10 years from now. Be able to explain the basis of your design and how it relates to the lifestyle you project.

3. Paintings, prints, and textiles are three forms of the visual arts. To get started, do one of the following: create an original painting in acrylic, oil, watercolor, gouache, or mixed media that expresses something about you and your life. Your painting can be a portrait or a landscape; it can be abstract or realistic.

   OR

   Create an original print (relief print, silk screen, lithograph, etching, or a mixed-media print) that can be used as a poster, a page for a calendar, or a greeting card.

   OR

   Create an original design for embroidery. Transfer the design to fabric for a pillow or wall hanging or to an article of clothing. Embroider your design.

4. Three-dimensional arts are those you can see from all sides, such as sculpture, mobiles, pottery, furniture, and some textiles. Choose a spot in your home, school, town, public building, or park that you feel might be enhanced by a work of three-dimensional art. Create the three-dimensional design full-scale or, if your choice is a large sculpture, make a small-scale model.

5. The music that particularly appeals to you may be the popular songs of today, Gregorian chants, opera, chamber music, atonal electronic music, jazz, folk music, rock, spirituals, or baroque music. For this activity, choose a musical form that combines with other arts: an opera, operetta, or musical. Listen to one of these on the radio or on a recording or watch one on television or in a movie. Then create a fun-time activity booklet or a puppet show that will help someone else learn about that particular work. Make suggestions for instrumental and vocal music in your activity booklet.

   OR

   Put on a performance for a group that explains a musical. Include music, both instrumental and vocal. The instrumental music can be either live or recorded.

6. There is more to theater arts than just acting. To find out about one aspect of the theater, explore the role of the mask. Why are the sad and happy masks used as a symbol of the theater? Look at the drama masks of the American Indian, ancient Greeks, and at African or Asian masks. Put on a dramatic reading or a playlet using masks. Be involved in making a mask of papier-mâché or other material and in staging or reading in the production.

7. Dance is a natural form of expression. Whether it's the exuberance of the current popular dance or the square dance, the quiet beauty of the ballet, or the exotic drama of the dance of some faraway countries, it can be participated in and appreciated by almost everyone. Here's a way to begin learning how to share dancing with others. Participate in a square or folk dance. Write down, draw, and/or record the dance steps so that you will be able to teach someone else. Now find a group to teach and get your students dancing, too.

OR

Plan a dance of any type in which some parts are danced by a group and some parts by individuals. Ask some friends to join you. Try out movements. Decide whether your dance tells a story or is just a plan in space. Then perform the dance and choreograph, or compose, it so others can do it, too.

8. The camera can be an artistic medium as well as the means of recording events and places. Photographs can be hung on a wall to enjoy as one would enjoy a painting. They can also tell a story. Create a photographic story on a theme of your choosing. Use at least eight photos to tell your story.

OR

Create a slide/tape presentation or a film that is intended to teach or present an idea to an audience. Your presentation should run at least two minutes.

9. In almost every country and every period of time, art forms have been created by people without formal art training. These are often called folk arts. They include woodcarving, basketry, pottery, weaving, spinning, quilting, embroidery, and furniture making. Start exploring the riches of folk art by finding examples or pictures and descriptions of five different kinds of baskets or pottery, either from other countries or from the United States. Choose one type of basket or pot and make a small sample basket or pot using the same method. Explain to others why you chose the one you did, and what materials you used and why.

10. Look at yourself in a full-length mirror. Think about what would look best on you. Is it stripes or plaids? going up and down or around? What color would be good? deep purple, brown, light pink? What about the fabric texture? heavy, nubby wool or smooth, draping polyester? all one color or a separate look? After you have made these decisions, design an outfit that reflects what you think would be best for you.

11. Interior design and residential architecture are to homes what fashion design is to a body. You use the same principles of color, line, proportion, texture, and harmony to create a pleasing and livable environment. To get a feeling about what is involved, do one or both of these activities.

Imagine you have only one room in which you must live, work, and entertain. You haven't much money to furnish it. Draw a plan for the room, including furniture you would buy or make. Indicate other aspects of the room: window coverings, fabrics, colors, floor coverings, and storage space.

OR

Plan your dream apartment or house by making a scale drawing of the interior on graph paper. Indicate doors, windows, closets, electrical outlets, and other standard items the way an architect would.

12. Every day you see around you ways in which art communicates a message. Create a poster promoting or advertising an artistic event, or design a package for Girl Scout cookies. In either case, use lettering and some other form of visuals for your design — illustrations or photographs, for example.

OR

Write a message. Write a poem, short story, speech, or article about the best book you have ever read.

Artistic Crafts

The artistic craftsman uses the principles of art and design to create objects of beauty in a variety of media. This interest project explores a wide range of artistic crafts. While these pieces can be made by the manufacturing process, artistic creativity is best expressed when these objects are crafted by hand.

Complete four activities, including the two that are starred.

1. Learn about the history of crafts in the United States — quilting, basket making, wood carving, making pottery. Look for the transition between folk arts and sophisticated crafts. Select a piece of folk art in one of the media. Investigate its history, its maker, and its use in society. Then find a work of the same medium created by a contemporary artist. What are the differences in design, technique, and cost, and in the training of the artists?

2. Investigate the place of the crafts in other societies. In many cultures, crafts are such an important part of the society that those who create them are revered as special people.

   Choose two countries and investigate the crafts and the people who make them. Be able to report what crafts are made in these countries, how they are used in the society, and the role of the artists who create them in the culture.

*3. In order to find out which media you most enjoy, experiment by making small sample pieces in four different media. Choose from leather, wood, clay, glass, metal, paper, or textiles and fibers.

*4. Choose one of the following crafts to investigate: leather working, metal smithing, macramé, decoupage, candle making, basketry, spinning and dyeing, stained glass, paper sculpture and origami, pottery, modeling, ceramics, quilt making, printmaking, wood carving, woodworking, mosaics, jewelry, enameling, puppetry, and mixed media. Then do the following:

   - Study the history and development of the craft in the United States and other countries.

   - Collect pictures of several designs in this craft.

   - Learn about the tools, equipment, and materials used in the craft.

   - Experiment with several ways to do the craft.

   - Design several pieces in this craft.

   - Make to completion one of your designs.

5. Look through books and magazines on interior decoration. Choose pictures for a scrapbook or make drawings of seven ways that artistic crafts such as pottery, basketry, weaving, quilting, and stained-glass making are used to decorate the design of the room. Show your collection to an art teacher or interior decorator and discuss the kinds of artistic crafts that are appropriate for different styles of interior design.

6. Visit a crafts show, exhibit, or sale, and do the following:

   - Find out how many different media are represented in the show or fair.

   - After looking at the objects on display, decide which ones you like best and why. Be able to explain the reasons for your preference to your troop or group.

   - Talk to one of the artists to find out:
   — how she or he got started
   — what kind of training was required
   — what part of her or his total income derives from sales

—what are the pitfalls and satisfactions of the artist/craftsman.

Give a report to your troop or group by means of a scrapbook, lecture, videotape, slide presentation, or audiotape.

OR

If you cannot visit a crafts show, exhibit, or sale, visit an artist/craftsman in her or his studio and ask the questions. Then prepare your report.

7. Choose one of the craft media that you know well enough to teach. Decide which Girl Scout age level the medium would be most appropriate for. Through your leader, group coordinator, or council liaison, arrange to teach the craft to a group of Girl Scouts of that age level. How well did they do? Perfect your lesson and offer to teach other groups in the council on call.

8. Many books, magazines, and crafts schools emphasize artistic crafts in today's society. Find at least five books that are on the subject of your major craft interest. Review them. List as many magazines as you can find that have articles on how to do different crafts.

Find out about at least three schools that offer courses, workshops, or degrees in the crafts. List the names, addresses, and major courses. Send for a brochure if they have one. Put all this material together in a file and share it with your leader, group coordinator, or council liaison.

9. Compare forms of fine arts, industrial arts, and artistic crafts that are part of our daily lives. First look at and collect pictures of some fine arts (painting, sculpture, architecture), industrial arts (cars, furniture, packaging, business interiors, appliances, etc.), and artistic crafts (pottery, weaving, quilting, etc.) Then write an essay comparing what you feel are the essential differences between the art forms and the importance of each in our society.

Creative Writing

This interest project will help you put yourself in closer touch with your feelings. You will express your creative abilities through several forms, or genres, of writing: journal, poetry, short story, and drama. You could start your own portfolio.

Complete eight activities, including the one that is starred.

1. Keep a journal for at least two months in which you write for at least 10 minutes each day. Express your thoughts, ideas, and feelings, and describe incidents or anything else that is meaningful to you. Your journal may contain poems, stories, drawings, quotes, or any other forms of self-expression. Date each entry and keep the entries in order in a notebook or folder. You may read one or more of the published diaries and journals of famous (or not-so-famous) people as a guide for your own journal.

2. With one or more other girls or by yourself, plan a story hour for young children, senior citizens, or another group in your community. Read aloud from the writings of your favorite author, or from your own writings. Or, put on a play for your audience. This can be an original script of yours, or a script that your group has written.

*3. Learn some of the important elements of literature. Read a variety of stories, plays, and poems on different themes. Notice how each writer develops the important elements: setting, mood, character, plot, language, conflict. Look up writing terms such as *metaphor, personification, simile, alliteration, dialogue,* and *foreshadowing,* and try to find examples of them in your reading. Write a short story, play, or poem using some of these techniques.

4. Sharpen your observation skills with this activity in sensory writing ("sensory" means involving the senses). Pick a location and spend fifteen minutes to a half hour concentrating on one of your five senses at a time. First write down everything you see. Then close your eyes and write down everything you hear. Try to be as perceptive as possible. Do the same exercise with your senses of touch and smell, if you can apply them to the location. Later, organize your notes into a poem, play, story, or composition. You may want to try this activity again at another time of the day or at another location.

5. Poetry is meant to be read out loud; very often, its sounds emphasize the meaning of a poem. Select an assortment of poems and read them out loud. You could also tape them and then listen to them. Learn what *alliteration, assonance, consonance,* and *onomatopoeia* mean. Find poems that apply these terms. Finally, write two or three poems using what you have just learned.

6. Try your hand at shaped verse or picture poetry. Here, you carefully select the length of each line so that it contributes to the shape you want your poem to have. After you have written or typed your poem in its final form, cut your paper in the shape of your poem.

7. Read literature from at least three cultures. Discuss your reactions with someone. Are they the same? How do they differ?

8. Write a children's story. Illustrate it with pictures or drawings. Read it to a young child or to a group of children, perhaps at a library story hour or a day camp.

9. Write a short story, poem, or play that takes place in a fantasy world. You can create a make-believe society or kingdom and characters with characteristics and talents much different from those of today's human beings. Your story could take place in the present, past, future, or in another dimension.

10. Select a one-act play and change it by rewriting the ending, adding another character, or changing the setting. In any case, the outcome should be quite different. Or, write a play using actual characters from history or literature. Place them in a different setting (or time in history) and create an interesting dialogue for them. This may be either a one-act or full-length play.

11. Write a segment for your favorite half-hour TV show. Remember to use all of the characters.

12. Explore some of the many different writing careers. Learn from your public librarian, teachers, and others who your local writers are. Try to meet one or two of them and ask them about their work.

13. Find out about copyrights: how to apply for them, how they protect you, how long they are in effect. Select an original writing of yours and apply for a copyright.

Fashion Design and Clothing

Fashion design can be an exciting career, but designing and making clothing for yourself and others can also be a life-long hobby. It can provide many satisfying hours, as well as provide you with a fashionable wardrobe at much less cost than ready-made purchases.

Complete eight activities, including the one that is starred.

1. Color is one of the most important aspects of fashion design. Not everyone looks good in every color. The colors you wear need to be suited to your skin, hair, eye coloring, and even personality. Here is an activity that is best tried with a group of friends.

   Collect pieces of fabrics about 20″ x 40″ in some pure basic colors — red, yellow, blue, purple, green, orange — and in black, white, and brown. Try to get some lighter, subdued tones of these colors as well; for example, pink, blue-green, beige, gray.

   Make a score sheet that includes the names of the participating girls. Have a numerical rating system for each piece of fabric. Have the group vote on which piece looks best on each person, and include this in the score sheet.

   Afterward, discuss why you think certain colors look best on some people. How will this knowledge affect your choice of clothing? Keep your own color chart to refer to when designing for yourself.

2. The fashions of any period of history say something about that time. In times of affluence, more fabric might be used. Skirts might be longer and fuller. In times of economic hardship or scarcity — for example, in time of war — less fabric might be used.

   Fashions change, but styles of dress that were once fashionable can become so again. Look through books and magazines that show women's fashions of the 1920s, 1930s, 1940s, 1950s, 1960s, 1970s, and 1980s. Can you spot any style that has come back? What are the changes from period to period in skirt length, colors, fabrics, patterns, touches of lace and bows, tailoring, etc., versus straight tailored styles? Document your findings with sketches and descriptions. Try to link changes in fashion to people or events of a certain period.

   Take one item of clothing, such as blue jeans, and list the changes in them in your lifetime. Are there any trends that you can list? Do they reappear in cycles? Based on what you have listed, predict the next trend for the kind of clothing you reviewed. Have several friends also make predictions. You might want to put the papers away for a year before checking to see who was the best spotter of trends.

3. Fabrics are an important part of fashion design. The wrong fabric with a good design can result in a useless outfit. A good fashion designer carefully selects fabrics to suit the design, the use to which the outfit will be put, and the season of the year or the climate in which it will be worn.

   Collect several fabric swatches. Be sure to include both natural and synthetic fibers — wool, cotton, linen, polyester, nylon, rayon, and combination. Note the feel and study the characteristics of each fabric — its thickness, warmth or coolness, texture, stretchability, drapability, whether or not it is wrinkle-resistant, etc. Mount the swatches on cards with their characteristics written on the backs.

4. The best fashion in clothing is that which fits the wearer. Your own measurements will be the basis for adapting or creating new designs for yourself. Make a chart that includes the following measurements: length from neck to waist; neck circumference; arm circumference and length; measurement of bust, waist, hips, thighs, leg. Use these measurements to analyze your figure type to purchase clothing and select patterns with such designations as Junior, Miss Petite, Misses, Woman, or Half Size.

5. Some basic principles can help us find appropriate designs for all figures. These principles are shape (as seen in silhouette), line, proportion, balance, rhythm, and emphasis.

Collect pictures of fashions that show the following:

- a variety of silhouettes — A-line, shift, dropped waistline, sheath, princess, tent, empire, etc. Include suits, dresses, and slacks.

- variety in the use of line — diagonal, decorative, horizontal, vertical.

- variety in proportion — e.g., relationship of jacket to skirt, collar to blouse.

- balance — symmetrical or asymmetrical balance. Where do closings come on a dress or jacket? Where is decoration placed?

- rhythm — dresses that repeat a design, or that have a "flow" (the fabric moves with the person wearing the dress).

- emphasis — a variety of points of interest; for example, at waist, neck, or hemline.

Organize your collection by file folders. After the collection is complete, select at least one example from each of the above categories and write an explanation of how that design principle relates to a body type or can camouflage figure defects. Choose the design elements you like best and explain why.

6. Creating your own personal style comes with experience. If you merely choose your clothing by what appears in the latest fashion magazine, an important factor is missing — you.

Create a chart for yourself that includes the following:

Lifestyle: Where or how I spend my time; for example, at school, at home, at work, at social affairs, in travel, on hobbies.

Preferences: Colors I like (e.g., reds, yellows, greens, and blues). The way I like clothes to feel — smooth, soft, crisp, etc.

Needs: Environmental and personal needs, including clothes chosen for warmth and coolness and those that bring out the good points and minimize the weak points in my figure.

Budget: After you have completed the chart, make a list of the clothes that meet your needs and preferences, check off those you already have, and make a plan for how and when your budget will accommodate the others. Don't forget to calculate how much of your clothing budget you can afford to spend on fads for the fun part of your wardrobe.

7. We can't always buy all the new clothes we would like, so part of good fashion design is adapting what we already have to look newer, fit better, or be more useful. Take a look at what you own and make a list of items you no longer wear for one reason or another. What could be done to make each garment wearable? A skirt is too long; can it be shortened? A dress no longer fits; can it be altered to fit? The colors on a blouse are not right for this season; can the garment be dyed? A collar is frayed; can it be replaced with another? Choose two garments, confer with your parents and your leader or consultant, and decide on adaptations to make the garments usable. After you have agreed on the changes, complete the adaptations.

8. Take a shopping trip. Explore the costs, quality, care, and design of clothing. Choose one type of garment to research, such as a coat, dress, suit, slacks, or jacket. Look for at least five examples of this item in stores or catalogs. Make a chart that compares design, color, cleaning and care requirements, fabric (including fiber content), and cost. Note the differences in the various samples you survey. Compare all the pros and cons of the samples on your chart, then decide which one you would buy, and why.

9. Make a list of all the possible careers you can think of that are associated with the creation of clothing and fashions in general, from the idea to the finished product. Show your list to friends, family, your guidance counselor, and others, and get their reactions. When you have listed as many careers as you think there could be, try to locate people in your community who have those careers. Contact one of them. Interview that person to discover how she or he became interested in such a career, what training is needed for it, and what are the satisfactions of the job. Ask if the person you interview can add to your list of clothing and fashion careers. Share your list and what you learned from your interview with your troop or group.

10. Fashion designers gain inspiration from many sources. Two of the most common sources are folk costumes and historical costumes, which include styles of dress — garments and accessories — and hairstyles.

In books, magazines, museums, or by contacting ethnic organizations, find several examples of authentic folk costumes from different countries. Sketch them if you cannot get pictures. Decide what feature — colors, fabric, a part of the costume, or an accessory — could be a fashionable part of a wardrobe today. Make one item and document what inspired it.

OR

Search through history and history-of-costume books, and visit museums or historical associations for designs from at least four periods. Sketch the designs if you cannot get the pictures. Using one or more of these as inspiration, create a contemporary design. Do a fashion illustration, including the color and fabric to be used. Tell what type of occasion your design is suited for.

11. Fashion illustration is a very special way of sketching and drawing. You use your skills as an artist, but you must do so in a way that conveys the look of the garment as accurately as possible.

    Collect from fashion magazines and newspapers several styles of fashion illustration. Which ones appeal to you and why?

    Sharpen your skills at drawing the female figure by taking a course in figure drawing, using a drawing instruction book, and practicing enough to be able to create a good figure drawing in several poses.

Then, create fashion illustrations of at least five outfits. Show them to your family, friends, or troop or group members and ask them to vote for the outfits they would be interested in, based on your illustrations. Find out the reasons for their selections to help you improve your illustrations.

*12. After you have done seven other activities for this interest project, use all the knowledge and skills you have attained to design and sew a garment for yourself. Choose colors, fabric, textures, silhouette, and design lines for your figure. You may use a purchased pattern, but make some changes so it is personally yours.

Folk Arts

Folk art is any type of art made by people without formal training in the arts. It is known as the art of the people. Folk artists are able to express their vision of beauty in a way that others can feel and appreciate. Everywhere you look, you'll find examples of folk art — from whirligigs on rooftops to decorated bowls, plates, and crocks in kitchens. Many pieces have a signature, design, or a form unique to a cultural, regional, ethnic, or religious group. That embroidered sampler your great-grandmother made, or that piece of whalebone scrimshaw carved by a sailor whiling away the lonely hours at sea — these and many other objects are now being recognized as valuable forms of artistic expression.

Maybe you've already begun to collect some olden-day objects, these everyday things of beauty — or their modern counterparts being created by people today. If so, this Folk Arts interest project could be for you.

Complete eight activities, including one of the three that are starred.

1. Interview someone who works in the folk art tradition today, someone who creates:

basketry	kites
beadwork	leather work
blown glass	objects out of natural materials, such as pinecones, shells, apples, and cornhusks
calligraphy (decorative writing)	
collages	
crocheting	papier-mâché
decorative knots	pottery
decorative paintings	quilting
decoupages	scrimshaw
dolls	tinware
embroidery	toys
furniture	weaving
	wood carving

You might ask the following questions:

How have techniques, designs, and styles for making the art changed? stayed the same? How traditional is the art? What has the artist changed or added to the traditional form? What does the artist think is appealing about her or his art? What market is there for this art?

If the artist has actual examples, illustrations, and photographs of folk art, you might ask to see them.

2. Explore the folk arts of your area by visiting a collection in the following: a private home; a city, state, or town collection; a historical society or a museum. Write a short article for a newsletter or newspaper about the folk arts in your area. Illustrate the article with photographs or drawings.

OR

If you are exploring folk arts in a group, have members bring in some examples for the group to enjoy. Discuss where each example came from, techniques used in making it, and why these examples appeal to you and to others. If the pieces are unusual and interesting, you might arrange to display the collection in a public place.

3. Make a collection to show the varieties of design found in one type of folk art, such as baskets, religious symbols, woven cloth, or pottery. If you can locate pieces made in other countries, you may even have an international collection. Use photographs or illustrations if you do not have examples of the actual objects.

4. Study one design element and gather illustrations, samples, or photographs that show this design element as it appears on many types of folk art. For example, choose a design of a flower, a geometric shape, a rising or setting sun, animals, hearts, or children. Show the design on quilts, in paintings, on jewelry, on rugs, in weaving, on beadwork, etc.

Using any one of these motifs in your own way, create an example in the folk art tradition.

5. Pick craft objects made in our time and identify the ones that you believe could be considered folk art in the future. Be ready to tell what qualities they have that might make them folk art, and try to tell something about the tradition that inspired them. As a group, what do the objects express about the culture? Which of the following objects might one day be considered within the folk art tradition? Which might not?

- leather belt decorated with stencils

- embroidery on denim vests

- record covers

- papier-mâché sculptures

- T-shirts with brand-name logos.

6. Interview one or more people who are attempting to preserve antique examples of folk art for museums, for profit, or for their own personal pleasure. Look over a collection and discuss the appeal of each piece and the techniques necessary to care for and preserve such art.

*7. Make an object in the folk art tradition that requires a painting technique. For example:

- birth and marriage certificates (which often employ a decorative-lettering technique called fraktur)

- boxes

- decorated tinware

- hex signs

- kitchenware

- painted furniture

- painted papers

- paintings.

*8. Using sculpture techniques, make some things in the folk art tradition. For example:

- carved figures

- ceramic ware/pottery

- decoys

- signs

- totem poles

- toys

- weather vanes or whirligigs.

*9. Make some things in the folk art tradition using weaving, stitching, knotting, or dyeing techniques. For example:

- baskets

- batik designs

- beadwork

- dyed or woven fabrics

- fancy knots or macramé

- quilts

- rugs (hooked or braided)

- samplers.

10. Hold a folk art festival. Invite local artists working in the folk art tradition to display their wares. Invite collectors to show and describe examples from their collections.

11. Collect illustrations, photographs, or samples of folk art particularly attractive to you. Once you have at least five examples, design a place in your home for the objects. You might plan a shelf, a corner, or a whole room. Draw a floor or wall plan, showing where each piece would be placed.

12. Teach a folk art technique or talk about folk art to a group of adults or children. Collect materials for the group's use and show simple techniques for producing the type of folk art you have chosen. Show examples to illustrate your ideas.

Invitation to the Dance

Dance is one of the oldest art forms. It is found in almost every culture and period in history. Dance represents an expression of human feeling. As an art, dance is an arrangement or pattern in space. It is also an arrangement in time, for it uses rhythm — audible, visual, or both.

Complete eight activities, including the one that is starred.

1. Design or select a warm-up exercise, aerobic dance, or jazzercise routine you can use to prepare your body for participation in a dance activity. Include exercises to stretch and strengthen the muscles and joints you will be using when dancing. You should know the purpose of each exercise and decide how long you need to carry out your routine. You also need to be aware of exercises that should be avoided. After you have practiced your routine, select a piece of music and perform your exercise to the music.

2. Learn five social dances, including three that were popular with your parents' or grandparents' generations. Although the development of social dancing is a fairly recent part of the history of the dance, it is an important way for people to meet and to enjoy each other's company. Be able to demonstrate the dances you have learned to others and explain something about how and when they came about.

3. Learn five American folk dances. Such dances are rich and varied and reflect the cultural traditions and customs of many people who came to the United States. Be able to teach the dances you learn to others and explain something about their history and background.

OR

With your troop or group or others who are interested, put on a folk, square, or country dance. Learn the dances first, select the music, designate a caller, find the space to hold the dance, issue the invitations, and have fun!

4. Learn about a dance from each of three countries that represent different areas of the world. Find out how these dances express something of the life, customs, and values of the cultures they represent. Teach or demonstrate at least one of the dances to a group. If possible, wear whatever would be traditional for this dance.

5. As a service to a group of youngsters, select several simple singing games or rhythm games to teach to Brownie Girl Scouts or other children. After they have mastered those games, choose one simple dance to teach them.

6. Develop an ice-skating, roller-skating, or gymnastics routine for a piece of music you have selected. Make certain that the movements of your exercise match the mood and tempo of the music. Determine how your routine is related to dance and in what ways it differs. Practice your routine and, if possible, perform it for someone else.

*7. See at least one full-length dance program live or on television. This could be ballet, modern dance, or ethnic dance. Note the important elements of the performance that distinguish this form of dance. Musical accompaniment, dance steps and motions, costuming, makeup, and lighting are all things to consider. Think of what you might write in a review of the performance and, if possible, prepare one for a school newspaper or a troop or council newsletter.

8. Take lessons in some form of dance. Practice so that you can dance in a performance for an audience. Afterward, demonstrate to a group of Girl Scouts some of the basic steps, customs, and history of your dance form. Be able to tell them something about the training, commitments, and rewards of being a dancer.

9. Compose (choreograph) your own dance. Listen carefully to different pieces of music and choose one for which you would like to compose dance movements. Use your sense of space and timing to arrange the pattern of the dance with music. Move to the music to create a dance pattern. Consider using some props to make your dance more interesting. Practice your dance pattern and then demonstrate it to someone else.

10. Find out about three famous dancers, past or present. Learn about the kinds of dancing they did, how they got started, and the training they received. Find ways to share what you have learned.

OR

Find out about three current careers related to the dance. Write up your information, following the format of *From Dreams to Reality: Career Cards.*

11. Explore the use of costume in dance. For many forms of dance, specific kinds of costuming, including footware, are important elements of the total performance. Find out about five types of dance that have traditional costuming. Trace the development of the style and, if possible, see these costumes firsthand. Share your findings with someone else.

12. Select a program of music for a variety of types of dances — ballet, tap, jazz, folk, social, dance of other countries — and present it as an entertainment for a group of people. Ask the group to guess the kinds of dances that would go with the music.

Museum Discovery

Museums are our link with the past and the future. It is in museums that we relive our past and enter into exceptional views of the present so that we may better plan for the future. A museum presents our heritage and our vision of the future. It is a celebration of human existence. It can be the place for you to explore an avocation or vocation in the arts, humanities, history, or science.

Complete eight activities, including the two that are starred.

*1. Make a directory of parks, museums, and exhibits in your area. You can get information about sites from a municipal office, chamber of commerce, arts council, automobile club, historical agency, travel bureau, arts and entertainment section in your newspaper, or your state tourism agency. Include local historical agencies, botanical gardens, zoos, arboretums, archaeological sites, cemeteries; exhibits in houses of worship, local industries, libraries, hospitals, and businesses, or exhibits in any other place in your community. Visit as many of your sites as possible. Make your directory available to other people.

2. Interview five professionals at area museums. You may find curators, educators, interpreters, development officers, administrators, public relations officers, registrars, museum shop personnel, conservators, exhibit preparers, naturalists, researchers, etc. Write up your information, following the format of *From Dreams to Reality: Career Cards.*

OR

Write a profile of five museum-related professions. You can look into these professions by writing to museums or universities or by reading relevant books at the library.

*3. Explore the possibility of providing service at a local museum, historical society, or library. Do they need ongoing service or help on a special project? You can help to fill that need by contributing your skills for a specific event, project, or function.

4. Develop an activity for other Girl Scouts based on the resources of local museums. You might plan activities such as:

- a field trip for Brownie Girl Scouts
- an orientation before a museum visit
- a crafts festival
- a historical reenactment
- a museum discovery day
- an arts project related to a museum collection
- a science museum overnight camp-in
- adopting a zoo animal
- adopting a building
- developing a junior museum association or becoming active in one
- attending a film festival.

5. Develop a mini-exhibit for your place of worship, school, Girl Scout council, library, or historical society. Exhibits could be about the following, for example: Girl Scout crafts; the history of your Girl Scout council, school, house of worship, or community; scientific processes or discoveries; collections owned by individuals in your area. Research, organize, catalog, and exhibit your chosen subject. Remember, it is important to care for objects and photographs responsibly while you are displaying them. Obtain written permission for the use of display items and research how to care for and exhibit each item properly.

6. Choose one type of object or material. Learn about how to care for it, and its origin or how it was made. The objects or materials can be seashells, paintings, textiles, papers and documents, photographs, fossils, animal skins that have been preserved through taxidermy, stamps, or anything else you are interested in. Develop a resource file about your material or object and offer it to a local museum or cultural agency.

7. Develop a public relations campaign to encourage Girl Scouts or other individuals or groups to attend museum programs, exhibits, or special events. Learn about successful advertising techniques from experts. You may find them at your local newspaper, a department store, an advertising agency, a printer or publisher, or a radio or TV station. Use your imagination. Apply what you have learned in your campaign. You may wish to include brochures, fliers, posters, public service announcements, press releases, or a publicity event.

8. Since most museum professionals have expertise in a special field such as local history, art, or natural science, have them share their knowledge. Invite a museum professional to make a presentation for your school, troop, or group. Be sure to tailor the subject of the presentation to the interests of your audience. You may want to include a museum professional in a career exploration event.

9. Explore ways that museums use new technology or trends to better serve the public or to preserve and exhibit their collections. Are they using computers or current conservation techniques? With the information you gather, write an article about the influence of new technologies on a museum in your area. Your school, council, or troop newsletter, your local newspaper, or a historical society publication may be interested in your article.

10. Originally, museums were created for the wealthy, but today they belong to everyone. Many museums, as public organizations, are trying to be accessible to people with disabilities. In what ways are museums in your area doing this? Add this information to your directory or resource file. (See Activity 1.) As a service project for an area museum, you may wish to volunteer to develop a resource for individuals with disabilities. Resources include taped guidebooks for the blind, guidebooks for the hearing-impaired, Braille and raised-letter labels, large-type exhibit labels, and outreach programs for those unable to visit the museum. Contact a community professional or an agency or association for individuals with disabilities for ideas and help.

11. Museums often use living history to teach us about individuals, events, or a way of life. For example, at the Juliette Gordon Low Girl Scout National Center, visitors can see a reenactment of daily life when Juliette Low was a girl. Participate in an established living history program at a museum or site in your area.

OR

Develop a presentation of your own that will add to a museum exhibit. You will need to investigate the specific details about your period, event, or individual. It can be fun creating an authentic period costume. Bring your characters, event, or time to life by performing for museum visitors or another group.

12. What kind of museum would you create if you had unlimited resources? Design your dream museum. Include architecture, location, collections, purpose, programs, staff, and resources. Make a model or drawing or write a proposal. Share your ideas with your family and friends. You may wish to display your model or drawing at a local museum or other facility or submit your proposal to an appropriate agency.

Music

Music is a universal language that most people enjoy in one form or another. It can sound joyous, lighthearted, sorrowful, dramatic, soothing, rollicking — pick the mood or feeling and you can probably find a piece of music somewhere that expresses it perfectly. Music can be plain fun for listening, dancing, singing, or playing, or it can be a serious profession. It can be termed popular or classical, but always music is reflective of many sources, many cultures, many inspirations. Most of all, it is a personal art — you as an individual responding to the sounds of the music you identify with.

In this interest project, you can learn song leading, sing or play with a group of friends, or investigate careers in music. For some of the activities, you will need to learn how to read music — if you don't already know how.

Complete eight activities.

1. Imagine that you are a radio disc jockey or are conducting a music-listening program in a library. Select some recordings and tapes for an interesting program. Plan what you want to say about each song and give your performance.

2. Background music is an integral part of film and other entertainment involving visual images. Listen to a few musical scores from movies, slide shows, or television programs. How does the music make you feel? Prepare background music to enhance a performance of your choice, such as a slide show, home movie, dance, mime, poetry reading, storytelling hour, or skating routine.

3. Jazz, rock, punk rock, disco, soul, salsa, gospel, country, and western music are just a few of the current music sounds. Choose your favorite and plan a program to share this music with others. Include examples that trace its evolution. Show variations in the music and the ways different musicians perform it.

4. Start a music group or join and make music with a vocal or instrumental group. Participate for a minimum of several months or until you give a performance.

OR

Study a musical instrument or take voice lessons and participate in a concert, recital, or performance for friends.

5. Play or sing a musical composition or song written before 1900 and one written since then. Explain how each one reflects the period when it was written. Improvise music in the styles of each musical period you selected.

OR

Design a record jacket for a musical composition or song written before 1900 and one written since then. Include something interesting about why or how the music was written. Share your finished product.

6. Learn at least five songs from among the following: action song, children's song, grace, round, two-part song, art song, folk song from your part of the country, folk song from another part of the country, song in another language, or song from another country. Teach at least two of these songs to someone else.

7. Learn song-leading techniques. Select several songs to teach to a group. Demonstrate your expertise by teaching a group the songs you have chosen or by leading singing at a songfest.

OR

Learn some basic conducting techniques. For practice, you can conduct while playing a record or tape. Show your ability by directing an instrumental or vocal group.

8. Share your knowledge of music with others by helping with music activities or lessons in your community. You might work with a young child, a group of children, adults, or at a hospital or community center.

9. Make up a tune of your own and play or sing it. Write it down if you can or have it taped. Share the tune with others.

10. Within every cultural group throughout the ages, music has had special meanings and has often been played on special instruments. There are marches; there are dirges; there is happy, dancing music; there is music for holidays, for game times, and for work times. Find someone who can tell you about the music and about the musical instruments of her or his culture. Learn that person's favorite songs and what the music means to her or him. Try to find the actual musical instrument(s) used or photographs or sketches of each one. Share what you have learned with others.

OR

Research music in a culture other than your own. Find out about the part music plays in that culture. Learn about this music and the instruments it may be played on. Prepare a visual display, give a presentation, or demonstrate with the use of instruments or records what you have learned.

11. Attend at least three different types of musical performances or concerts wherever they might be held — for example, a concert hall, stadium, school, house of worship, community center, or club. Do one of the following: Before or after one concert, interview one of the performers. Ask the person how she or he became a part of the group, what special training she or he has had, what music she or he performs or composes, and what music she or he likes best.

OR

Play the role of a music critic and review a performance for a school or local newspaper or for a class.

12. Make several folk instruments, including one in the percussion, woodwind, and string families. Then give a workshop to show a group how to make at least one of these instruments. Help them use the instruments in group singing or other musical activities.

OR

Visit a person, shop, or factory to see how a musical instrument is made or repaired.

OR

Observe a piano or organ tuner at work. Ask about the materials, tools, skills, and techniques needed in the job.

The Performing Arts

Do you love the sound of applause? Does the thought of appearing on stage set your heart racing with anticipation? Or are you a reluctant performer who prefers being in the audience? In either case, activities in the performing arts may be for you. This interest project will give you a chance to explore the excitement of entertaining through theater, music, or dance.

Complete eight activities.

1. Performing involves conveying a message through sight and sound. Facial expressions and body language can be important techniques of the art. Practice performing in front of a mirror. You might tell a joke, act out a story, sing, or dance. Pay particular attention to body movement and facial expressions. Keep a record of your daily practice sessions, noting techniques you have discovered to help convey emotions.

2. Much of the effect of a performance can depend upon illusion created through staging. Design a stage setting and then make a diagram for each scene showing where tables, chairs, and other props will be placed, and where the characters will stand or sit.

3. Sharpen your appreciation skills by learning more about an art form that interests you: for example, instrumental music, vocal music, theater, the dance. Find out about its history. What are considered classics in the form and what direction has the art taken in the last 30 or 40 years? Compile your information into a booklet or presentation for younger children. Use this information in completing Activity 10.

4. Attend three live performances or watch three of the following on TV or videotape: a dramatic play, a comedic play, a musical comedy, an opera, or a ballet. Be able to answer these questions: How are setting, lighting, and music used to convey mood? How is the plot developed and how are the characters developed? What symbols, action, or music are used to create suspense or give comic relief? Use this information when completing Activity 7.

5. The performing arts require years of study and preparation. Find out where advance study is available for the art form that interests you. Find out proficiency levels necessary for admission, audition requirements, fees, scholarships available, and age requirements. Talk to or write to a professional artist about her or his preparation. Find out what advice this artist would give a young performer. Share your findings with your Girl Scout troop or group or family and friends.

6. Each of the performing arts has a professional association, guild, or union. Frequently, professional performers must be union or guild members to be able to work. Find out about membership requirements for your local chapter of the American Federation of Musicians and Actors' Equity.

7. Develop an original solo performance in your art form. Create a musical composition for one instrument or write a dramatic monologue or choreograph a dance. Perform your creation before an audience.

8. Perform an original or established work with a theater, music, or dance group (it may be a community or school group or a Girl Scout troop or group).

9. Develop a guidebook for girls interested in your art form. Include information about where to master the art, professional associations, careers in the art form, and tips on producing a performance.

10. Teach a group of younger children or older adults about your art form. Involve them in a performance. (See Activity 3.)

11. Find out about copyright protection for original work, what the benefits of copyrighting are, and how the material is registered. Register your original composition.

12. Find out about careers that use an art form in ways other than performance. For example, many therapists use music or dance as part of their treatment of patients. Find out about the preparation needed for these careers and where to find opportunities for employment. If possible, observe someone practicing in one of these fields.

Photography

A blank piece of white paper floats in a tray of liquid. Suddenly, eyes, a smile, the outline of a face appear on the paper. It's not magic, this "painting with light." It's photography, the art of creating images with light and chemicals. It can be done with a simple $10 camera or a sophisticated $1,000 camera.

To become a good photographer takes time and practice. This project will help you learn the basic technical requirements of photography, so that you'll be able to communicate through visual images. Don't get discouraged if everything you try doesn't look good the first time. You'll develop ways to control those "happy accidents" and turn out the kinds of pictures you'd like, time after time.

Complete eight activities, including the starred ones. Most activities include two options, and you should choose one to fit your interest levels.

*1. Simply put, every camera is a "box" with a hole in the front to let light in. The light reflected by whatever is put in front of the hole carries the image to a piece of film or paper coated with light-sensitive chemicals. The paper or film is placed opposite the hole in the box.

The first and most important step in photography is learning to operate a camera successfully.

EITHER

Start by using a simple or automatic camera. First, read all the directions and become familiar with the basic language of photography. Next, practice holding the camera steady, looking through the viewfinder, pressing the shutter release, and advancing the film. When you are comfortable handling the camera, buy a roll or two of film. Then, load the camera and take some pictures.

OR (ADVANCED)

If you want more control over your picture taking, learn how to operate an adjustable camera. On an adjustable camera, show how and when to change the lens opening, shutter speed, and focus settings. Examine cameras that accept different lenses. Learn how to

put the lenses on and take them off a camera. Learn how each one affects the pictures you take. Find out about different film sizes, speeds (ASA), and types. Figure out which films your camera will take and which your budget can afford.

2. Shadows can be mysterious, funny, solemn, serene... and they can create stunning graphic effects.

EITHER

Photograph shadows that occur naturally or that you create. Move around to experiment by taking pictures with light coming from behind the subject (backlighting) and with lighting coming from the side (sidelighting).

OR (ADVANCED)

Show how to expose for highlights and shadows. Learn what light-exposure meters do and how they work, then practice taking readings. Set the ASA on a meter or on a camera with a built-in meter. Try bracketing exposures; that is, take three pictures of the same thing, one at the indicated exposure setting, another at a lens opening one stop larger, and the third at one stop smaller. Write down the exposure settings and look for the differences in the pictures when they're developed.

3. The light available for a picture is not always what you want. Many times you may need to supply your own lighting.

EITHER

Learn how to use a flashbulb or an electronic flash.

OR (ADVANCED)

Arrange a visit to a photography studio to see a demonstration of different lighting techniques, such as direct, bounce, rim, or pinpoint lighting. Ask the photographer about tenting, the use of umbrellas, and how putting different diffusion materials in front of light sources creates different qualities of light.

4. Focusing is one of the most important elements of photography. This activity will help you learn how to focus on subjects at different ranges.

EITHER

Most simple cameras can't focus at close range. Take pictures of the same scene, experimenting by moving closer to your subject (the foreground may be out of focus). Notice the difference in the pictures and discuss how you could use other focusing to get special effects.

OR (ADVANCED)

Experiment with "depth-of-field" (the range of what's in focus). Take several pictures of the same subject from the same distance, fairly close to the camera, but change the lens opening each time. Record your settings for each picture. Look at each picture to see what's in focus and what's out of focus. Compare your pictures and figure out how different settings for depth-of-field can add to a picture's impact. Look through photography books or magazines for more pointers about depth-of-field.

5. You may not always want a sharply defined picture. The soft edges of blurred and diffused images can also create moods for you.

EITHER

Get a soft look with a simple camera. Try taking a picture: (1) while you're moving the camera to follow a moving object (panning); (2) shooting through frosted glass; or (3) of a reflective surface, such as water.

OR (ADVANCED)

With an adjustable camera, experiment with slow shutter speeds and slow film to produce a softened image. Talk to an experienced photographer about setting your camera to get a sharp, candid shot quickly. Try capturing some action yourself.

6. Changing your point of view can create pictures that say how you feel. Imagine how tall a tree would look if you took its picture as you lay on the ground and shot straight up the trunk to the very top.

EITHER

Take pictures of one subject from four or five different vantage points. Choose the one picture that most clearly shows how you feel about the subject. Show your pictures to others and find out if they react the same way.

OR (ADVANCED)

Invite a newspaper photographer or other photojournalist to speak to your group about photojournalism, including photo essays. Then take a series of photographs that tell a story from a special vantage point. For instance, you might help increase public awareness of barriers to people with disabilities by picturing steep stairways or doors inaccessible to wheelchairs. Or you might take pictures from a toddler's eye level to show hazards such as dangling cigarettes and chair corners.

7. Fascinating abstract images can come from using common objects for casting shadows or from using a flashlight as a paintbrush.

EITHER

Find out how to make a picture with shadows on light-sensitive paper (a shadowgraph or photogram). Arrange and combine objects to block out light and form "white shadows." Try moving the objects or changing the lights to get different shading effects.

OR (ADVANCED)

When is a flashlight a paintbrush? When you turn off all the lights and move the flashlight in front of an adjustable camera with its shutter open for about two minutes. Set the camera on a tripod or table where it won't move and don't advance the film until the shutter is closed. To produce some eerie and interesting effects, have someone pose in front of the camera in the dark, then turn the flashlight on your subject for about 10-15 seconds. Turn off the flashlight while your subject moves to another position, and then shine the light onto her or him again. Let your subject move one more time. Then close the camera shutter and switch on the lights. The result will be a picture with three images of your subject on it. Experiment with this technique; use the flashlight to "paint" in the air or photograph a slow-moving subject for a ghostly effect.

*8. Plan a portrait of a group of friends. Before you take the picture, go to a photography exhibit or look through photography books or magazines for pictures of groups of people. For your group picture, try to visualize what your friends think about each other and who they are as individuals. What do you want the picture to tell about your friends? Ask your friends what type of place they think would be good for a group portrait. Plan where you'll take the picture. Keep in mind that you can arrange this group any way you like. Use everything you know about the visual arts — lines, perspective, space, rhythm, and texture — and take more than one picture so you can decide on the best set-up. Pay special attention to the effects of light and background on different skin tones. Once the pictures are developed, discuss them with your friends. Have you pleased all of them?

*9. To become a photographic print, the exposed film in your camera must be developed and printed. You can develop the film yourself or have someone else do it for you.

EITHER

Explain how to select photos from a contact sheet and how to give instructions to a lab for cropping and printing. You might ask a photographer, photo-lab person, or school newspaper or yearbook editor to demonstrate how she or he uses contact sheets.

OR (ADVANCED)

Arrange to visit a darkroom at a local newspaper, school, or friend's house to watch someone process film and make a print. Be able to identify the equipment and chemicals used in developing a roll of film and in printing a picture. Record what you've seen and heard so you can do it yourself. Process a roll of exposed black-and-white film and print it yourself.

10. Learn how to mount, mat, or frame photographs attractively. Keep a record of any special information about each photo (who, what, when, and where, lighting, film type, camera setting, etc.).

EITHER

Put together an album or portfolio of your photographs and show it to others. Try to have one of your photographs printed in a school or community newspaper, yearbook, magazine, or other publication.

OR (ADVANCED)

Enter a photography exhibit or arrange for your photographs to be displayed in a bank, a library, a gallery, a fair, or other public area. Choose a theme for your exhibit or have each exhibitor in your group choose her or his best shots for display. Invite parents, friends, teachers, newspaper editors, community officials, and anybody else who might be interested, to a reception to view the photographs and talk with the photographers.

11. Combine your expertise with the wide-eyed enthusiasm of children.

EITHER

Borrow or buy simple cameras so that you can teach photography to children. Show them how to hold the camera steady, look through the viewfinder, press the shutter release, and advance the film. Have them practice before you put film in the camera. Then take them for a walk. Play some visual sensitivity games with them as you go. Stimulate ideas by suggesting that the children take pictures of objects that begin with or look like a certain letter, are pieces of bigger things, or look hot, cold, soft, hard, smooth, or rough. Have the pictures processed and talk about them with the children. Ask the children to make up titles for their photographs.

OR (ADVANCED)

Show a child or a group of children how to make and use their own pinhole cameras or plan a one-day photography workshop for them.

The Play's the Thing

The theater has always held a fascination all its own. The suspense, the romance, the comedy, the tragedy, the intrigue have appealed to generations of audiences. The theater, in some form, can be found in almost every historical period and in every country.

The theater arts can include everything from costume making to lighting to stage managing to public promotion of a group's production, in addition to the performing aspects. This interest project will give you an overview of these arts and skills.

Good live theater is happening in all parts of the United States — in schools, colleges, and community theaters that are relatively inexpensive but still very professional. See as much live theater as you can. Learn to be an appreciative and discriminating audience.

Complete eight of the following activities, including the one that is starred.

1. See at least two theater productions, amateur or professional. At least one of these should be live. The two plays should be different types: a tragedy, a comedy, a farce, a musical, an opera, a historical drama or pageant, or a presentation of selected scenes or dramatic readings. Prepare a written or tape-recorded review of each show, as if you were the drama critic for a school newspaper, a radio show, or a TV news show. Include the following elements in your review:

   • the type of production

   • the names of the cast and the name of the director

   • a brief description of the plot or story

   • your evaluation of the quality of the production, including all production elements — acting, costumes, sets, sound, lighting

   • whether you recommend that your listeners or readers see the production.

*2. Become involved in putting on a dramatic production before an audience, such as a school group, a religious group, or a theater group in your community. The production should have scenes or sequences, sets, costumes, makeup, lighting, sound, props, and publicity. You could participate as one of the actors, as an assistant to an adult director, or by helping with any other aspect of the production. Keep a journal or log of your experiences. Include something about the overall production, as well as the specifics of the jobs you did.

3. With a group of three to five friends, select three types of material that lend themselves to reading aloud without the need to memorize. These could be one-act plays, poems, short essays, or selected scenes from plays. Read and rehearse your three selections together. Assign parts to each other and arrange the timing of a 40- to 45-minute presentation. Then offer the program to a group of people: for example, a group your own age, younger Girl Scouts, a parents' group or club, or senior citizens, depending on which group you feel is most appropriate for the material you have chosen.

4. Dramatic presentations offer the viewer a variety of human emotions. Creative dramatics help you learn to express those emotions spontaneously, without learning lines. With a group of your friends, prepare and present at least two creative dramatic games and/or improvisations. At least one should be in pantomime.

   Here is an example of an improvisation. One person reads a short paragraph describing a certain situation —who, when, where, what is happening, etc. The actors and actresses then create a short scene about that situation.

   Here is an example of a dramatic game. Divide into three teams. Two teams write up real-life situations on cards. These teams exchange cards and take turns acting out the situations in pantomime. The third team tries to guess what the situation was. Variations of these techniques could be used for your own creative dramatics presentation.

5. Prepare a list of dramatic presentations combined with such other art forms as music, dance, visual arts, film. Then view at least one such presentation — an opera, for example. Prepare an outline of a dramatic presentation you would like to give and how you would do it. If possible, carry out your plan.

OR

Find out about the growth of the theater from early Greek plays through medieval miracle plays, Elizabethan drama, and theater in eighteenth- and nineteenth-century America to contemporary theater. In some visual way, share your findings about the ways theater arts have changed over the decades.

6. Read at least two one-act or full-length plays to get an idea of how plays differ from stories. After this preparation, choose a short story, a short folktale, or a situation you have made up yourself and write it in play form with characters, lines, and stage directions. Share your play with someone who is interested in the theater for her or his reaction.

7. Puppetry is one form of dramatic art. Learn about three types of puppets — hand, rod, and shadow puppets, marionettes, etc. Find out about the history of these puppets, countries where puppetry is popular, and the kind of staging needed for different kinds of puppets. Choose one type of puppetry and, alone or with some friends, make the puppets and put on a short puppet show for an audience.

8. List five ways you might be able to give service in your community with the skills you have acquired in dramatics. Then choose one to carry out. Discuss the project with the possible recipient of the service. Some examples might be helping another Girl Scout group put on a play, earn a badge, or do an interest project related to dramatics; storytelling at a day-care center, nursery school, or library; or putting on a play at a senior citizens' center.

9. Portray a character in a play. For every scene in which you appear, write up the character analysis, including how you look, dress, and walk, and your emotional and motivational objectives. (Why are you there? What do you want?) Learn about the importance of warm-up exercises and of training in voice and dance. Read at least one book on acting. Know about the Stanislavsky method.

OR

Find out about some of the great actors and actresses, both past and present. Use live theater, movies, or TV to see as much as you can. Share your findings in an appropriate way: for example, a scrapbook or a timeline poster with pictures or drawings, dates, etc.

10. Learn how costumes and makeup combine to help an actor or actress bring a part to life. Some of the things you should find out about are as follow: designing, altering, and fitting costumes; selecting accessories; using makeup to create a sense of youth or age, good or evil; techniques for applying makeup for stage, TV, film, or opera. Become involved in this aspect of a dramatic production by working on actual costumes or makeup. Make a drawing of one complete costume or demonstrate one complete makeup task to others.

OR

Find out about costumes from different periods of time. Make a scrapbook of pictures or drawings from plays and/or operas of various periods or eras. Design one costume for your scrapbook. Tell what fabrics you would use and what play the costume is for.

11. Help design and make a set, including props, for an actual production. Lighting is one of the aspects you should consider, since much of a dramatic production depends on lighting changes to convey mood, intensity, or emotion. Prepare a report on what you did, including some actual drawings or sketches, what materials you used and why, visual effects created, cost estimates, special skills needed, the time it takes to build a certain set, and how a timetable is set up for a production from design to the opening of the show.

OR

Choose a play and design the set for that play, including all of the above elements. Share your plan by creating a model of the set for one scene and explaining the specifics of materials, cost estimates, and time estimates as above.

12. Find out about careers behind the footlights or behind the scenes. Some places or people to turn to for information would include drama schools, little theater groups, and professional trade associations, such as Actors' Equity and the American Federation of Musicians. Interview someone involved in an aspect of the theater that interests you to find what education and/or experience is needed for her or his job. Create a skit, career cards, or a recruitment flier to share your findings about that job.

Prints and Graphics

The first prints were made centuries ago. The techniques have improved, the equipment and materials have become more sophisticated, and, today, prints and graphics are all around you, from books and magazines to museum works of art. This interest project will help you learn more about this fascinating subject.

Complete seven activities, including one of the three that are starred.

1. The lettering on a poster, greeting card, or advertisement can make an important difference in its eye appeal and readability. Look through books and magazines to find several type styles. Clip or photocopy these and keep them in a notebook.

   With this information, design a greeting card or a poster (8½″ x 11″ or smaller) using press-on lettering, hand lettering, or stencil lettering *and* a black-and-white illustration. The illustration can be hand-drawn, clip art, or an uncopyrighted illustration. Make a copy of your greeting card or poster on a duplicating machine. Show it to your friends or troop or group and ask them to rate its effectiveness. If it was not effective, try again.

2. The study of print techniques can take us back to early civilization and into many cultures. Choose one of the following types of prints to study: stencil, silk screen, woodblock, engraving, etching, lithograph, aquatint, mezzotint. Research the history and variety of that art form. When and where did it start? Does the technique vary from one country to another? What artists have worked in the medium? Collect some examples of the art form. Prepare a display about your print for people to see.

3. The products of printing and graphics are all around you. Prepare a list of careers you think might be associated with printmaking in some form. Confer with an art teacher, guidance counselor, or other adult knowledgeable about the arts and review your list; add or subtract until you have a list of careers involving prints and printmaking. Interview someone in one of the careers on your list to find out what education is needed, what the job entails, what special satisfactions or considerations it offers. Report your findings to your troop or group.

4. One of the great advantages of prints is that you can make more than one copy from the original. For this reason, prints are a perfect art medium for greeting cards, invitations, posters, and advertisements. Design a print, decide the print medium you wish to use, and make copies for your troop or group. You might want to design a piece for a cause that needs promotion in your council or community and offer it as service project.

*5. Relief prints involve a process in which only the raised part of the surface — the part *in relief* — prints. Relief prints can be created with a variety of materials — erasers, linoleum, and wood, for example. Each medium requires its own type of equipment. The choice of a material for a relief print should be based on your printmaking experience. If you are a beginner, choose an eraser, a potato, or a material such as cardboard. If you have made eraser prints, move on to linoleum and other materials. Study the technique, history, and art of the print type selected, including how to make prints of two or more colors. Design and create a print.

*6. Stenciling and silk screening are printing techniques based on the same principle. Study the history and techniques of these print forms. Collect some samples and be able to explain the technique and equipment involved, including how to create a print of two or more colors. Create an original design in stencil or silk screen.

7. Designs on fabric are created through many printing techniques. Clothing, table linens, curtains, and hangings are a few examples of printing on fabric. Textile printing can also be accomplished on ready-made items, such as pillowcases and T-shirts. Relief prints, silk screens, stencils, and other types of prints can all be used for textile printing. The inks used and treatment of fabric after printing must be of a type that will permit the fabric to be washed or dry-cleaned. Also, the design must be suitable for the fabric and its use. Create a design for three of the following:

- place mats

- curtains or draperies

- summer skirt

- decorative accessory (picture frame, book cover, etc.)

- child's bedspread.

Then choose one of the three, study the type of print needed for your design, and execute your print on a piece of fabric. Learn about the chemicals and solvents used in the printing process. Make sure you choose non-toxic products and use a work space with adequate ventilation.

8. Find out about artists who have worked in a print medium — block printing, silk screening, etching, engraving, stenciling, lithography, or mixed media. Research at least three of these artists and be able to do a presentation about them. Include the following information about each one:

- the artist's life and career

- the print medium the artist worked in

- examples of the artist's work, with a simple description of how this type of print is made.

9. Seeing is believing. We can often find out more about how something is made by actually seeing the finished product than by just reading about it in a book. Take one of these trips and make a report on it to your troop or group:

- Visit an art museum or gallery to find as many examples of prints as you can. Collect postcards of a few examples, if possible.

- Visit the studio of an artist, a commercial studio, or a printmaking class in a college of art to observe an artist and/or printmaker at work. Find out all you can about the printmaking process you are observing.

- Visit a commercial printing plant. Before you go, read up on the printing processes that will be used.

*10. Monotypes, lithographs, collotypes, etchings, engravings, transfers, roller prints, silk screens, rubbings, and press prints are all types of prints. Learn about and experiment with one or more of these types and create an original design.

11. One of the best ways to learn something thoroughly is to teach it to someone else. This activity involves being familiar with a print medium, knowing how to teach it, and knowing something about the age level of the students. Prepare a lesson on printmaking for younger girls. Select the type of print medium appropriate for the age level, and prepare a list of materials and methods of teaching. Check with a leader, group coordinator, or art teacher to make sure you are on the right track. Give your lesson to a group of the age level represented.

Visual Arts

All the arts are a way to communicate, to learn, to "see," and to discover. Even if you say "I can't draw," you can enjoy the visual arts, cherish a sense of beauty, and value the talents of others. Whether you want to appreciate the expressions of others or create your own, whether you're the sender or receiver of a visual message, your role can be an active one. With your eyes, your mind, or your hands, you can explore new forms and colors.

This project focuses on the visual arts — those that appeal to sight. These include paintings, sculptures, textiles, designs, buildings, pottery, furniture, and many everyday objects.

Complete eight activities, including one of the three that are starred.

1. Find at least 10 forms of visual art in your community. Collect pictures, or sketch or photograph the pieces of art, and put these in a collage, a display, or a scrapbook. Explain your collection to others, including why you consider your choices works of art, what functions, aesthetic or practical, they serve in the community, which one is your favorite and why. Ask others to explain their favorites and their reasons for selecting them.

2. Take a trip to an art museum, historical museum, restored building, village, or to someone's home in your community. Before going, find out something interesting about the place you have selected. While you are visiting, keep a log or sketchbook, take pictures, or buy postcards. After you return, create a visual record of your experience or describe your impressions.

OR

Become so familiar with a collection or museum that you can create a tour for others. Consider the special needs of the group; for instance, children, people with disabilities, or older people. Decide which works you would show them, what you would tell them about the artwork, and how long the tour should take. Plan ways to balance activities to avoid fatigue and boredom. Check the plan with your leader or council representative and, if possible, conduct the tour yourself.

OR

Plan an "art trail" through your community with stopping points where art objects may be seen: pictures in banks, murals in public buildings, sculptures in parks, displays in gift shops, etc. Be a guide or prepare a written guidebook to your trail.

3. Select one period, style, or school in the history of art, such as medieval art, impressionism, or cubism. Look through books with lots of pictures of your chosen style. Then put together a scrapbook of pictures or sketches of that period with titles and artists. Explain in your book where each piece fits as part of the life or culture; what kind of group created the works of art; how the art related to other factors in world history at that time; and if the works foresaw things to come. Imagine yourself in the setting you've chosen and create your own piece of art that reflects the spirit of that style.

4. Specialize in one art form by looking, absorbing, and looking some more. Pick a few examples from a medium, craft, or profession such as painting, sculpture, cartooning, architecture, textile design, furniture making, printmaking, pottery making, or photography. Discover all you can: look for something new and wonderful, or seek something different about your old favorites. Collect information from books, museums, magazines, artists' studios, auctions, collectors, or anywhere!

Share your knowledge in a demonstration, talk, visual presentation, or display for the benefit of others. Include your findings on:

- how such works of art are designed and made

- the people, past or present, who created your examples

- what these art forms are like in other countries, other parts of this country, and other periods of time

- someone who is working in this art form in your community. Interview or write to that person to discover how she or he works. why this medium? What preparation has the person had? What is satisfying about her or his chosen field?

5. Design is all around you, in nature and in objects created by people. Start a design notebook. Include pictures or drawings that emphasize a particular element or principle of design — line, shape, texture, color, space, pattern, rhythm, balance, and movement. Think about how the creator arranged elements into designs to use in fabrics, buildings, stage sets, etc.

   Select several objects that you think are well designed and describe why you chose each one. Experiment with creating several designs of your own — a page of designs based on color combinations, another of textures, another with motifs repeated to form patterns.

OR

How does the spiral shape of some shells relate to a spiral staircase? How could the bark of a tree relate to a woven drapery? Choose natural objects, such as shells, leaves, or rocks, and show how the patterns in these objects could have influenced designs made by artists. Influenced by the natural objects you have chosen, create your own visual work of art.

6. Look around for some everyday examples of what art does. Then create some artworks to show how visual art can tell a story; promote a product; illustrate a story, magazine article, or poem; decorate an object; be worn or used.

   Without saying what their purpose is, show your creations to someone, such as your consultant. If she or he can tell what your intention was, you have communicated your message through art.

7. Use your talents to create an original fashion design for yourself or someone else to wear every day, for a special occasion, or for a theatrical production. Sketch the design as a fashion illustration or actually make it. Include explanations of fabric, color, and why this is a good design for the person and the occasion.

8. Brainstorm with someone else and list all the careers you can think of that relate to the visual arts. The obvious careers are as a sculptor and painter, but try to include others not so obvious — window decorator, greeting-card illustrator, maker of museum dioramas, gallery curator, or museum docent. Talk to your family and teachers about other suggestions and then look into as many job categories as you can. Interview or write to people to discover how they found out about their jobs; what training or experience they had; what advantages and disadvantages are related to their jobs. If at all possible, arrange a short apprenticeship in a career of your choice.

9. In books, prints, or at a local museum, select a work of art by a known artist that seems especially expressive to you. Figure out how the artist has composed the elements to communicate the feeling. In a painting, drawing, or sculpture, create a work that expresses something you feel deeply. Show the artwork to others.

*10. Create an original work of art in any two-dimensional medium of your choice. You might work on a painting, a woodblock, or a lithograph, in pen and ink, or in silk screen. Learn the procedures and try individual ways of handling a medium. Learn about the chemicals and solvents used in your medium. Make sure that you choose non-toxic products and use a work space with adequate ventilation.

*11. Create an original work of art in any three-dimensional medium of your choice. Make a composition in space using materials like wood, clay, soapstone, metal, or sculpture compound. Show that you understand that what "isn't there" — space — is important in sculpture. Show that you can use the tools safely. Wear protective clothing and eye wear when necessary.

*12. Create an original work of art in a craft medium of your choice. Use your own design sense as you work in textiles, paper, metal, wood, clay, leather, plastic, or mixed media.

Weaving

Weaving is one of the oldest and most universal crafts. People have been weaving since prehistoric times, even in the most primitive of cultures. Remnants of cloth woven thousands of years ago show the skill and creativity of ancient weavers as they made everything from functional items to beautiful works of art. This craft is still practiced in many forms today. So, explore the intricate and interesting world of weaving and fibers — clothing, containers, and decorative arts in all materials imaginable.

Complete eight activities, including the one that is starred.

1. Visit a textile mill or chemical plant where fabrics are made or visit a weaver, weaving guild, or historic site to see a loom in operation. Interview at least two individuals about the production of cloth, using the format of *From Dreams to Reality: Career Cards.* You may find, for example, weavers, pinners, chemists, engineers, administrators, historians, and designers.

2. Visit a fabric shop. Before you go, make an appointment to talk to a staff person about the properties of various fabrics. Collect samples of wools, cottons, linens, silks, and man-made fibers such as polyesters and nylons. Make a file folder of these samples, noting the special properties and care of each. Natural fibers — silk, wool, cotton, and linen — undergo extensive preparation before they are ready for spinning. Investigate one natural fiber, actually participating in the processing, if possible, and add the in-depth information to your resource file. In the resource file also include samples of the various fibers in their raw state, if possible. Share your findings with someone.

3. Fibers must be processed to produce a thread or yarn before weaving can begin. Man-made fibers and silks are produced as thread and need less preparation before weaving. Other fibers, like cotton, linen, and wool, must be spun before weaving. Make a simple drop spindle and experiment with twisting wool into yarn (you may need to clean, card, or comb your wool).

OR

If there is a spinner in your area, visit her or his studio and observe spinning firsthand. You may wish to find out if you can take some lessons in spinning. Interview the spinner about her or his craft following the format of *From Dreams to Reality: Career Cards.*

4. Although part of the intricate beauty of a woven article comes from the weaving itself, the use of colors can enhance that beauty. Before the development of synthetic dyes in the early nineteenth century, people used natural materials for a range of hues. Indigo for blue and madder and cochineal for reds and oranges were highly valued. Other natural materials are readily available — for example, onion skins (yellow), marigold (yellow), azalea leaves (gray), berries (red), dandelion roots (purple), goldenrod flower (yellow), walnut or pecan shells (brown), white birch (yellow-brown). Synthetic dyes are also available.

    Complete a dye project. Use natural and synthetic dyes on unfinished, uncolored material or yarn and compare the different effects. Share your results with others. You may wish to use the materials you have dyed for a weaving project.

Warning: Dye projects are messy and permanent. They can also be dangerous if materials are not used properly and according to instructions. Be sure to prepare a safe work area with good ventilation and to wear protective clothing, including a mask and rubber gloves. You must use special utensils and containers for all dyes. Do not use kitchen containers or utensils again for food preparation. You will probably find it most convenient to work outdoors.

5. Some forms of weaving, such as card weaving and finger weaving, do not require a special loom. Investigate various kinds of loomless weaving and prepare a simple project using a technique of your choice. Teach this technique to a group of younger Girl Scouts or schoolchildren.

*6. Simple weaving can be executed on a loom you make yourself. Make a cardboard, wood-frame, inkle, backstrap, or other simple loom and carry out one of the projects listed below. Experiment with two of these techniques — plain weave, tapestry, or rya knots. Remember, use of color can make a simple project more exciting.

   • On a cardboard or wood-frame loom, make a pillow or wall hanging.

   • On an inkle loom, make a belt, a guitar strap, or a bellpull.

   • On a backstrap loom, make a belt or strips for a bag.

7. Most weaving is executed on looms with multiple harnesses. The more harnesses, the more complex the pattern produced. Looms can have from 2 to 24 harnesses. Select one of the following projects and complete it on a two-harness loom. You may have access to a two-harness loom through local schools, your Girl Scout council, a weaving guild, or an arts group.

   Weave a rag rug or a striped scarf or an ikat project, predying your yarn before weaving, or a set of patterned place mats or napkins.

8. Formerly, a standard home loom or business loom was a four-harness loom. This loom allows a great deal of versatility in weaving patterns. Explore different patterns of weave, such as satin, twill, summer and winter, crackle, huck, and overshot. Make a sampler using different weave patterns. Using a pattern of your choice, make a shawl, pillow, table runner, place mats, small coverlet, or other item.

9. If you wish to continue as a serious weaver, you will need to learn to warp and maintain a loom. With the help of an experienced weaver, learn to warp the loom of your choice. If no weaver is available, you can learn to warp a loom from a book; but, as always, it is easier if you have an experienced teacher.

10. Once your project is woven, it will need to be finished. Many other handwork techniques are used to add the final touches to a project, like knotting, crocheting, embroidery, and stitching. Investigate finishing techniques and choose one to finish one of your weaving projects.

11. Weaving is also used to make baskets. Investigate different styles and materials used in basketry. Assemble a file of your favorite styles and materials, including special reference to natural materials available in your area. Choose one style and material to become familiar with. Make a small basket using your chosen technique and materials. You may want to investigate learning basketry from a basket maker in your area. Basket making is an intricate and involved craft in its own right. Many craftsmen find it to be fulfilling and enjoyable work.

12. Spinning and weaving are so closely associated with the basic human experience that many folk, nursery, and popular songs refer back to this work. "Pop goes the weasel" is itself a spinning expression. Because of the rhythmic nature of spinning and weaving, these art forms lend themselves to the composing of work songs. Research and collect music relating to textile work and prepare a program of the music for your troop or group, other Girl Scouts, your school, or a local arts group.

13. Because weaving is universal, there are many kinds of textiles from ancient times to the present, and from many cultures worldwide. Survey international, historical, and contemporary textile collections in your area. Collections are owned by museums, galleries, houses of worship, businesses, governments, and private individuals. Add your findings to your resource file and share them with others. Go to see as many textiles as possible. You may wish to share your findings by planning a field trip for other Girl Scouts, your family, or friends.

The World of the Out-of-Doors

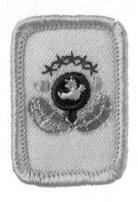

What is it that:

- molds and unites a group, and provides time to laugh together?

- mobilizes your muscles to paddle, pull, push, hike, hold on?

- challenges your abilities to think clearly, to plan for a safe journey?

- tempts you to see where a path or stream goes, or where the current will take you?

- uses the skills of a whole group — navigator, humorist, planner, leader, songster, and follower?

- challenges you to be observant and wonder why a lichen survives on a harsh rock surface, but not in polluted air? how a tall tree anchors itself in shallow soil?

- lures you to the top of a hill in the predawn chill to watch the sunrise?

It is the World of the Out-of-Doors. This world provides you with all these opportunities and more.

Complete eight activities.

1. Design a puppet show, an interpretive trail for a day camp, a wide game for a troop, a film story, or a canoe trail to tell others why clean water is vital for life. Use local examples to show all the things that water does: how plants and wildlife use and conserve it; the sources of water, including how and where it flows, and what it carries along; the difference between a wetland and a watershed; how nature purifies and removes wastes from water. Don't forget to portray the beauty of various bodies of water.

2. Winter snow and cold sometimes inhibit people's planning for outdoor activities. But winter is a time when woods, fields, and hills take on a special beauty in their white coats. Plan a winter hike, an overnight, or a snowshoe or skiing trip to take a special look. Discover for yourself how snow and other natural forces change the shape of the landscape. Look for the tracks of animals that climb, that hop, that have hooves. Look for the gnawings of porcupine, beaver, deer, rabbits. Find out how the winter inhabitants tap into the high-energy food sources in seeds and nuts. Enjoy the shapes of trees, rocks, clouds, and weeds. Find a way to share your discoveries with others.

3. Trace a part of the trail or course that American Indians, explorers, settlers, or merchants used to reach your community. See if you can find evidence of the modes of transportation that they used. Figure out the relationship between the local geography and the way people and goods moved through the area. Find a way to share this part of your community history with others.

4. Explore a nearby community, follow a bike trail, chart your own route for a biking adventure, or lay out a bike route for others to follow. Whichever cycling adventure you choose, know how to take care of yourself and your equipment, be familiar with bicycle regulations in your community and your state.

5. There is a thrill in learning to communicate with your horse, whether it is in a ring, on a trail ride, or a pack trip. Western or English? It's up to you. Get in touch with groups in your community who own or have access to horses and are knowledgeable about them. Ask the group to help you develop or perfect your riding skills. Take part in a trail ride, plan a series of short rides on trails or bridle paths, participate in a horse show, or attend an exhibition of Western or show riding.

6. Become a whiz at preparing tasty meals for yourself and your group to suit the different outdoor adventures you have planned. For example, plan a high-energy, no-cook meal to eat along the ski trail, or a gourmet meal served in style at your campsite. Plan and prepare three or more different meals in the open to complete this activity. Use a portable stove for all of these meals.

7. A good way to see the unspoiled beauty of the natural world is to backpack. Prepare a plan to update your camping and safety skills, and your physical endurance. Carry out your plan, culminating in a backpacking trip.

OR

Prepare an exhibit, based on your experiences, showing the personal and group equipment, and the supplies needed by a party of eight for a weekend backpack trip. Indicate changes (if any) for a week-long trip. Share this information with a group of less experienced backpackers.

8. Orienteering is an organized sport that uses a compass and map to get participants from one place to another in the shortest time possible. Orienteering is also an outdoor survival skill, which anyone going away from traveled highways should master. Test your ability with compass and map on familiar ground before you start bushwhacking through unfamiliar territory. Invite a consultant to help your troop or group become proficient in the use of a compass and in map reading, or use some of the resources for the Orienteering interest project on pages 138–139 to develop a game to interest others in orienteering.

9. On a map of your area, locate navigable rivers, lakes, ponds, and other waterways. Indicate small-craft landings, campsites, and canoe liveries. Navigate at least one of these waterways, keeping a log of the trip to share with others.

OR

Select or make a canoe paddle appropriate for your use. Design a personal symbol for it to identify it as yours. Add other symbols to the paddle blade or shaft to record your participation in canoe trips, canoe meets, or games.

10. Figure out ways to make it easier and faster to move a canoe, rowboat, or sailboat through the water. Try feathering your oars or paddle, sculling with a single oar, or trimming your sails. Show that you can propel your craft if you lose an oar or paddle, or if the wind dies.

11. While on an outdoor trip, take time to look at and enjoy natural textures, colors, symmetry, silhouettes, and shadows. Learn to use a magnifying glass, binoculars, or a telescope to add new dimensions to your world. Keep a log of the things you learn about your environment by seeing, hearing, smelling, and feeling. You may discover ways to:

- read cloud patterns to forecast the weather

- tell the prevailing wind direction by the shape of the plants

- tell about the activities of wildlife from food or tracks left behind

- tell the difference between the sounds birds make as notes of alarm and those for defending nesting territories.

12. Camp maintenance is a year-round job. Who is responsible for the jobs that must be done to keep your Girl Scout campsite or a nearby park in good condition? Do you know what you, as a user, can do to care for the equipment and site you use? Talk to the person in charge of maintenance, or check for yourself the many kinds of jobs to be done or the special skills needed to do the work. Find out what kinds of jobs you or your troop or group can do or learn how to do. Agree upon a time to do a "contracted" job of volunteer site service or take part in a scheduled workday or work camp to maintain the site.

OR

Vandalism is defined as the willful or malicious destruction or defacement of property. Often it is a simple and thoughtless act, such as carving initials on a picnic table or misusing a campsite. Find something at a camp or in your community that has been vandalized, such as a tent marked with graffiti, a defaced bus stop, or destroyed vegetation. Decide how long it took to vandalize this and why you think it was done. Then estimate the cost and the amount of time it will take to have the damage repaired, replaced, or removed. If possible, help with the repairs or develop a way to prevent future vandalism.

Animal Observation

Many people are fascinated by animals in the wild. Some study large species such as the grizzly bear or mountain lion while others are intrigued with tiny creatures of the insect world.

Watching wildlife can be physically demanding, intellectually challenging, and emotionally satisfying. You can watch animals during daylight hours or under the cover of darkness. Your observations can be made in a large metropolitan area, in a town woodlot, the backcountry of a national park or forest, or in your own backyard.

Many questions still remain unanswered about the life histories of animals. Important contributions have been made by amateur wildlife observers. You can make discoveries too! You may develop direction toward a career choice or you might begin a lifetime hobby of watching animals in the wild.

Complete eight activities, including the two that are starred.

1. Walk through a vacant lot, city park, or town forest. Stroll at a relaxed pace and return home. Jot down or sketch every detail that you can remember about your walk. What did you see, hear, smell, or feel? Return again the next day and walk the same route more slowly. Take careful notes. Compare. What did you observe this time? Did you find things you missed recording on the first walk? Try this exercise again in another natural setting to increase your powers of observation.

*2. Practice taking field notes. Select an animal to observe. Record the date, time, location, and weather conditions. Take careful, detailed notes to describe the animal you watch. What does the animal look like, what is it doing, what does it eat, how does it move, and how often does it move? Try different methods of recording your data until one suits you best. Try making sketches or taking photographs to supplement your notes.

3. Many animals survive as a result of their ability to remain undetected by their predators. These survival skills include protective coloration, remaining motionless, and hiding. As a technique for watching wildlife, practice remaining motionless. Look for a place that has signs of wildlife activity. Find a hiding place and conceal yourself. Try not to move. Await the presence of an animal. Describe what you saw. Did the animal see you or seem aware of your presence? If so, what was its reaction?

4. Many animals are shy and secretive. Others hide during the day and are active at night. Very often, tracks or signs of such animals are more evident than the actual animals. Learn to recognize five animal tracks. Follow the trail of an animal in the mud, sand, or snow. Study the trail and determine whether the animal was walking, running, or being pursued by another animal. From the tracks, try to reconstruct what the animal was doing.

OR

Begin a reference collection of tracks. Cast at least three animal tracks in plaster or take photographs of the tracks.

5. Show others how to look for evidence of wildlife. Plan a hike. In advance, establish at least eight "stations" along the route that illustrate signs of wildlife such as nests, holes, dens, droppings, or chewed nuts. See if others can find additional examples of wildlife signs.

6. Binoculars are an important tool for a wildlife observer. Learn to select binoculars for the purpose of looking at animals. Compare brands in a few price ranges. Find out what is meant by the terms *magnification, objective lens, field of view, alignment, resolution,* and *center focusing.* Try several pairs of binoculars to see how each pair suits you. Examine the manufacturer's warranty. Decide which pair you would purchase and be able to explain why you made your decision.

7. Animals can be attracted to feeding stations, bait lures, and artificial houses. Do at least two of the following and keep careful field notes about what you did and what animals you attracted:

- Set up a bird-feeding station and replenish the food regularly.

- Erect a birdbath and keep it clean and filled.

- During the nesting season, put out cotton, yarn, and hair on shrubs and bushes. Conceal yourself and carefully note what animals use these materials.

- Experiment with several types of bait lures and see what animals you attract. Put out bait stations using the following ingredients:
  — overripe pears and bananas mashed together
  — canned dog or cat food
  — rolled oats and peanut butter.

- Clear the ground around each bait station so that animal tracks can be identified.

- Wet down some soil to create an artificial mud puddle. See what butterflies are attracted.

- Put up several birdhouses. Find out the nest box dimensions and entrance hole sizes for the species you wish to attract.

8. Be able to explain what is meant by *hibernation* and *estivation*. Observe a species that hibernates or estivates. Be able to tell about its life history. Carefully observe an animal that hibernates or estivates. Note when it disappears and when it reemerges to resume its normal activities.

9. Animals can be disturbed by humans watching them. Choose an animal that you are interested in observing. Seek advice from a wildlife biologist or naturalist to learn what types of human behavior or intervention could cause the animal distress. Share what you have learned with your troop.

10. Visit an ocean, a lake, a pond, or a stream. Collect some aquatic animals and place them in a white basin filled with water. Identify at least three animals and learn for each:

- how it breathes

- how it moves

- where it lives (on the surface of the water, in the mud, attached to a rock, etc.)

- who or what eats it

- what it eats

- how it reproduces.

When you are finished, return the animals to the water.

*11. Wildlife observation can lead you into unfamiliar territory. Learn to use a map and compass. Demonstrate your ability to read a topographical map and to follow a compass bearing from a map. Be able to identify the poisonous plants and animals in your area. Show that you know proper dress and footgear for a day of wildlife exploration in all types of weather conditions.

12. Contact a local wildlife agency, bird club, or nature center. Participate in a project to rehabilitate or reestablish a wildlife habitat such as tree planting, erecting wood duck boxes, building den or nest boxes, or cleaning a section of a stream or vacant lot. Involve Girl Scouts in your neighborhood in the project.

13. Find out which colleges offer degrees in wildlife management and natural history interpretation. What are the admission requirements? What courses are required to obtain a degree? Visit a nature center or a wildlife refuge. Arrange to shadow a naturalist or a wildlife biologist for a day to learn about the duties of her or his job.

Backpacking

You are an experienced camper and it's time for a new adventure! Backpacking can provide ways to see beautiful backcountry areas, have fun with a group of friends, and have a special feeling about yourself, your skills, and your accomplishments.

Backpacking has become a popular recreational activity and many more people are using trails and campsites today than ever before. For this reason, each person must make a personal commitment to minimize her impact on the natural areas she uses. Learn and practice the ethic called "minimal-impact camping" or "no-trace camping." Use these tips as you plan and carry out your trips:

- Schedule your trip at times when sites will not be crowded.

- Hike and camp in a small group of 4 to 10 people; plan a stay of no more than one or two nights at each campsite.

- Use established trails and switchbacks to reduce off-trail erosion.

- Package your food in sturdy plastic bags and carry out all trash and leftover food.

- Select a campsite that has good natural drainage and where you will not crush delicate vegetation. Check overhead for dead trees.

- Use a backpacking stove wherever possible to minimize the use of wood. Destroy the evidence of fire scars. *Note:* Many areas no longer allow the use of fires.

- Use tents and clothing in colors that blend in with the environment.

- Wear soft-soled shoes or sneakers around the campsite to avoid crushing plants with heavy hiking boots.

- In mountain meadows, spread out and use different routes. Enjoy, but don't pick, the flowers.

- Dig a cat hole less than eight inches deep and at least 100 feet away from a body of water to use as a personal toilet. The organic soil will decompose human wastes.

- Wash clothes, dishes, and yourself at least 100 feet from water sources. Use biodegradable soap.

- Leave dogs and portable radios at home. Enjoy the peace, solitude, scenery, and wildlife of the area.

- Never feed wildlife. Enjoy observing animals and treat them with respect.

- Inspect your site carefully before you leave. Have you removed every evidence of your visit?

- To learn the skills for minimal impact camping and apply them in more challenging settings, see GSUSA's new slide/audiocassette production "From Backyard to Backcountry: Camping Lightly on the Land."

Complete eight activities, including the six that are starred.

1. Find out about the variety of backpacks and frames available today. Choose one that adjusts to fit you. Be sure it includes padded shoulder straps and a padded hip belt. Learn how to adjust, pack, and lift your pack. Weigh your fully loaded pack in preparation for each trip to make sure it does not exceed 20 percent of your ideal weight.

*2. List the items of equipment and clothing for a backpacking trip. Remember to include items to protect you from the weather — heat, sun, cold, moisture — and insects. Learn about the ways to maintain your body's internal environment by the use of appropriate clothing, food, and water. Talk with an experienced backpacker or read a book about lightweight backpacking to learn all the ways to reduce the size and weight of the items you take.

*3. Learn about the most common water pollutants in the area where you will be hiking. Learn about the various methods of water purification for backcountry areas. Use the ones that are best for your trip. Camp away from the water's edge so your activities will not pollute the water.

4. Help to plan the food for at least one backpacking trip. Learn about lightweight foods, those that pack best and last without refrigeration. Discuss which foods will provide the energy needed for the trip. Repackage foods to leave excess packaging at home. On your trip, practice ways to keep your food away from animals.

*5. Learn about the variety of backpacking stoves available. Choose one with butane or propane fuel to use on your trips. Read the operating instructions carefully and review them with a knowledgeable adult. Learn to operate the stove safely. Learn how to pack and clean it, and to dispose of the fuel canisters properly. Prepare a meal on the stove in preparation for a trip.

6. Assemble a lightweight first-aid kit for a small hiking group. Learn the first-aid treatment for burns, cuts, blisters, sunburn, heat exhaustion, heat stroke, hypothermia, shock, insect stings, contact with poisonous plants, and a bite by any poisonous animal endemic to your area.

7. Learn to use a compass and read a topographical map. Trace out a hiking route on a topo map. Tell what you would see and experience along the way by visualizing the terrain from the map symbols. Learn to gauge distance by the length of your pace and by the time walked. (See Orienteering, pages 138–139.) Write out a plan for what to do if you or your group become lost.

*8. (a) Choose and break in hiking shoes or boots appropriate to the trails you will be hiking. Learn proper foot care, including what socks to wear.

   (b) Take a hike of at least two miles with your pack loaded for a trip.

   (c) Take other hikes as necessary to condition your legs and cardiovascular system for the backpacking trips you have planned. Discuss with your hiking group the strengths and body limitations of members of the group. Learn the signs of fatigue and what you can do to avoid it.

*9. Show that you understand the principles of minimal-impact camping in the following ways:

   • by your choice of a campsite

   • by your choice of equipment and clothing to blend in with the environment

   • by proper disposal of human waste in a cat hole; by carrying out all trash; by proper disposal of wash water away from water sources

   • by the use of backpacking stoves; or, where appropriate, by using small, safe cooking fires and then removing all traces of the fire site

   • by maintaining the solitude and unspoiled nature of backcountry areas.

Describe other ways you can minimize the impact of your group on the sites and trails.

*10. Plan and carry out two backpacking trips of at least three days each. Obtain permission for each trip and the area where you plan to camp. Submit a written plan that describes the route, emergency procedures, group safety rules, equipment, menus, and who is participating. Explain why a group of 4 to 10 people is most appropriate in a backcountry setting.

11. Join a trail maintenance or campsite cleanup effort for at least one day.

OR

Keep a journal or create a photo essay about your backpacking experiences. Show or publish your work to help others understand the beauty of the wilderness, the need to protect backcountry areas, or the meaning of these experiences to you.

Camping

This Camping interest project will help you to progress further in outdoor living. You will be challenged to use, adapt, and expand the outdoor knowledge you already possess. Enjoyment in the out-of-doors depends upon being prepared, so increase your skill level and be sure to follow the standards of leadership and health and safety outlined in *Safety-Wise*.

As you plan your outdoor adventures, carefully consider the weather, the setting, your companions, and your activities. Pack for comfort and good times. Take care of your basic needs for food, water, shelter, and rest. Consider and care for the natural environment. Practice minimal-impact camping techniques. Make necessary reservations and arrangements for transportation well in advance and evaluate your experience afterward.

Complete eight activities, including the three that are starred.

1. Plan and carry out ways to vary your camping experiences. Extend your range. Backpack, bicycle, ride horseback, canoe, sail, ski cross-country, or find some other new and exciting way to get to the campsite of your choice.

OR

Camp in a different setting: a tropical climate, snow, mountains, desert, or in another country. Or choose another special setting that challenges your group.

*2. Learn to use a compass and to read a topographical map. Measure the length of your pace and show that you can judge distances. Demonstrate your navigational ability by planning and leading a day hike. Be able to explain what steps you would take if you became lost. (See Orienteering, pages 138–139.)

*3. Prepare and file a camping-trip plan with responsible persons, both in the area where you will be camping and at home. Find out about and list local emergency procedures such as for fire, flood, and lost or injured campers. Know where to get help. Show that you can recognize, set up, and respond to international distress signals. Assemble a basic first-aid kit and show you know proper treatment for bleeding, shock, cuts, burns, and insect bites, as well as hypothermia, heat exhaustion, heatstroke, sunburn, and frostbite.

*4. Practice minimal-impact camping techniques. Show that you know how to care for the environment when you select a route and a campsite, and as you meet your needs for water, shelter, food, and fire. Learn how to purify water for drinking. Dispose of waste in ways that minimize pollution. Set an example for others by using backpack stoves in wilderness settings, staying on the trail, and picking up trash.

5. Plan a well-balanced menu for a three-day camping trip for your group. Will you be camping in the desert or cross-country skiing to a campsite? Consider caloric requirements to meet energy needs as well as the weight and bulk of the food and what means of disposal you will use for garbage. Experiment with a combination of dehydrated/freeze-dried foods, convenience foods such as soup and gravy mixes or instant rice, and dry and fresh foods. Be careful not to take foods that will spoil. On the trip, be able to cache food away from animals.

6. Practice cooking by several methods. Small wood fires may be used for cooking if the site has sufficient firewood. Cook over a small fire, charcoal grill, and butane or propane backpack stove. Be able to start, keep burning, and extinguish the type of fire or stove for the meal you select. Also, try some preparations without "cooking" such as smoking, marinating, or cleaning and preparing raw foods.

7. In order to keep outdoor gear in good condition, show that you know how to help with the careful repair, maintenance, and storage of items such as tents, canoes, and backpacks. Make a piece of equipment such as a day pack, stuff bag, pack cover, vest, or sleeping bag. Weigh the advantages of making the item from scratch or utilizing a commercial kit containing instructions and precut materials.

8. Promote emotional well-being by figuring out ways that each person on your camping trip can help build group spirit. Be aware of your personal reactions. Keep in touch with the feelings that come from living and working together in the out-of-doors by recording your thoughts in a journal or sharing them with a friend.

9. Being prepared for changing weather conditions is important for the success of any camping trip. Before leaving, check the current forecast to make sure you have the proper clothing and equipment. Learn to read a weather map. Show you understand the significance of a barometer reading, wind direction and speed, and patterns of weather movements typical for your region. Record weather observations for a week before your camping trip and make a weather prediction. Note the weather conditions during the trip and compare them to your prediction.

10. Camp along a historic trail or follow the path of an explorer. Read accounts of those who blazed the trail. Trace the impact of humans on the area as you travel or at an archaeological dig site. Get in touch with groups that are interested in historic and natural preservation. Find out about their activities and participate in some of them.

11. Share your interest in outdoor living through a slide show, videotape, film, newspaper article, picture story, or collection of writings, drawings, photographs, or posters. Include sounds and songs from the out-of-doors by using tapes of nature's noises in the morning or at night. Work with your Girl Scout council or service unit to promote your message.

12. Plan and conduct a weekend camporee, a habitat improvement project, an outdoor day for younger girls, or an outdoor skills course.

13. Locate and list public and private recreational areas where you can camp. Help evaluate a site for possible use by other Girl Scouts. Talk with people who manage natural resources, or who provide camping programs, facilities, or equipment. Join with those people on a cooperative project such as skills training, career exploration, trail or campsite maintenance, environmental conservation, or a field trip.

Cycling

Pedal power is in! Americans are turning to bicycles for transportation, recreation, and exercise. If you are interested in joining the "pedal power" movement, there are a few things you first need to know. Most of today's bicycles are sophisticated vehicles. You will need to spend some time getting to know your bicycle. You should know how to ride your bicycle before starting this interest project.

Complete nine activities, including the five that are starred.

*1. Get to know your bicycle. Visit a bicycle shop and/or invite a cyclist to your troop or group meeting to help you become familiar with the different parts of a bicycle. Learn how to choose a bicycle that will properly fit your body and the type of cycling you are going to do. *Note:* There are different bicycles for racing, touring, rough terrain, etc. Learn about dressing properly for the type of cycling you are going to do. Learn about the equipment available for bicycles and cyclists—for example, helmets, chafing pants, car bicycle carriers, high security locks, panniers, toe clips, gear mirrors, reflective vests, and legbands.

2. A cycling session should start with a warm-up and end with a cool-down. The warm-up time is used to limber up your body through the use of stretching and moderate exercise. The cool-down time is used to stretch out the muscles again. Develop a warm-up and cool-down program that you can use with your cycling sessions and then demonstrate your program by leading others in the exercises. Remember to do these exercises "slow and easy"!

3. Help an interested group of younger Girl Scouts develop a plan to complete the Sports badge.

4. Many books and magazines and some videos and films are available on the sport of cycling. Explore the history of cycling, including the role bicycles have played in transportation over the years and how bicycles used in the past differed from those of today.

OR

Investigate bicycle touring, the story of America's participation in Olympic cycling, etc.

*5. Prevention can be the best medicine. Learn what you can do to help *prevent* the following: numb fingers and toes, hypothermia, boils or painful pimples in the crotch area, backache, aching wrists, weakness in the knees, sore muscles, dehydration, sunburn, chafing, etc.

*6. Cycling is a safe sport if you know your equipment, keep it properly maintained, and follow safety rules. However, accidents do occur. You should be prepared to treat any injuries that may occur with cycling. Know and demonstrate first aid for at least the following: heat exhaustion, abrasions, sunburn, broken limbs, spine and head injuries, bleeding, heat rash, hypothermia, chafing, muscle soreness, sore feet, sore buttocks.

OR

Take a course in standard first aid and personal safety, and cardiopulmonary resuscitation.

*7. Demonstrate your ability to do the following:

- Know, understand, and comply with the vehicle codes for the state in which you will cycle.
- Know and demonstrate hand signals. Contact the police department or local bicycle clubs to help you with these.
- Plot a course, using a road map, and follow it.
- Demonstrate the principles of cycling in traffic to a group of younger girls.

*8. Demonstrate a thorough knowledge of bicycle repair, including repairs to the following: tires, braking system, wheels, spokes, hubs, derailleur, headset, stem, handlebars, seat, and power train.

OR

Attend a clinic on cycle maintenance and repair. Demonstrate your ability to set up a maintenance schedule for your bicycle and stick to it. Demonstrate your ability to change a flat tire.

9. Tools are essential to bicycle repair. Know what these tools are and how to use them. Make a personal tool kit to carry on your bike at all times.

10. With others, plan a trip using your bicycle and camping skills. Be sure to include the following in your planning: council permission, activity checkpoints as outlined in *Safety-Wise*, clothing considerations, camping equipment, interesting rest stops, menus with high-energy foods, points of local history and lore, health history and examinations for all participants, how to get medical assistance while on the trip, filing a written itinerary with the base camp or with local authorities, minimal-impact camping procedures, and securing the necessary permissions as required by law.

Remember to stay away from main highways.

11. Try two of the activities listed below. At least one should be something you have not done before.

- bicycle touring
- cycle camping
- bicycle motorcross
- an indoor velodrome
- a scenic bicycle trail
- a triathlon, or some other form of bicycle racing.

12. Find out about the United States Cycling Federation's national world and Olympic team selections for women. Obtain a schedule of these events and see if you can attend one of the trials as an observer.

OR

Find out when cycling events will be on TV and watch with other cycling enthusiasts. Videotape portions, if you can, and look for championship form. Set some goals to be a winner yourself.

13. Add to this bicycle safety checklist and use it each time before you get on your bicycle:

- Check pins, bolts, and nuts for looseness.
- Check tire inflation.
- Check the pedal spindle to see that it is locked against the crank.
- Wear a bicycling helmet.

Eco-Action

Clean air, clean streets, clean water — these are banners being waved by environmentalists and ordinary citizens alike. But, just how do you get clean air, clean streets, or clean rivers? And why should anyone bother?

What does environmental impact mean? And what do you have to do with the balance of nature? How do humans fit into environmental systems?

Just one environmental upset like pollution can kill — plants, fish, animals, birds, and even people. Obviously, that's one reason why people are alarmed. But environmental awareness starts before the sensational. It touches the everyday quality of life of all people: as you breathe, eat, drink, get around, make things, use things, and throw things away.

Quite often, there are differing viewpoints as to what is or is not an environmental problem and what the solution, if any, is to be. Keeping up with current information and understanding all points of view on an issue are important, as is looking carefully at your own values.

Eco-Action is the Girl Scout name given to efforts to keep up the quality of your environment. Through this interest project, you will learn that environmental quality just doesn't happen and that choices need to be made by each of you in order to maintain a healthy living space.

Complete eight activities, including the one that is starred.

1. Find out what happens to the trash that leaves your home. Is any of it recycled into new products? If possible, visit the disposal site. Find out how trash is handled. How long will it take the various kinds of trash to break down (biodegrade) and be recycled by the environment?

2. Arrange to visit an air-quality monitoring station. Observe the kinds of measurements that are taken. Find out how air quality affects your community and your health. What does the term "airshed" mean? Find out how plants and trees can affect air quality and how air pollution affects them. For instance, how is a tree like an air conditioner? Ask what you can do to improve air quality and commit yourself to doing something about it.

3. Find out how waste water from your home and community is treated. If cesspools and septic tanks are used, find out how they work and what you can do to make them more efficient. If a waste-water treatment plant serves your area, arrange a visit to find out how it operates and what you can do to help make cleaner water. Find out the beneficial uses of sewage, such as for fuel and fertilizer.

4. Record some pleasant, relaxing sounds and some sounds that make you feel uptight. Share your findings with others and exchange ideas with them on ways to minimize annoying or harmful sounds. Find out how loud sounds affect human hearing. Does your community have a noise ordinance? Does it need one?

5. List the renewable and nonrenewable resources you have consumed within a typical 24-hour period. Categorize each of the resources as essential to survival, necessary for the maintenance of your lifestyle, or a luxury. List alternatives that you could use to reduce the waste of nonrenewable resources. Learn about the consumption patterns in the United States compared with other countries in the world. Find out how worldwide organizations such as UNICEF are working to bring about a more equal distribution of our natural resources. Learn about organizations that have a global concern for environmental problems.

6. Identify the major areas of environmental concern in your community, such as garbage disposal, water pollution, preservation of natural or historic landmarks, or lack of public transportation. Find out how local, state, and federal laws affect the environmental quality in your area, and who is responsible for enforcement of these laws. Are these laws being observed and enforced? Attend a meeting of a group responsible for making or enforcing environmental ordinances in your area. Explore a career possibility that links the environment and the law.

7. Trace the contributions of someone deeply concerned with environmental quality. Find out how this person became interested in environmental problems and how she or he pursued her or his interests.

8. On a map, locate all the recreational areas in your community. Are they convenient to all the people in your community? Do they provide recreational possibilities for the many different interests in your area? Find out where people in your community want and need more recreational facilities. Contact your local parks and recreation department to learn about its future plans. Arrange to work with the department on developing or renewing a recreational area in your community. (See Activity 5 in the Child-Care project.)

9. Monitor a stream for pollution sources and erosion. Learn to identify the plants and animals that are typically found in clean water and in polluted water in your area. What happens to the plants and animals that cannot adapt to the changes caused by pollution? Find ways you can improve conditions for wildlife and recreation. Develop a plan to improve conditions and put your plan into action.

10. Conduct a picture, poetry, or essay contest. Invite people in your community to submit entries expressing their feelings about environmental quality in the community. Set rules and deadlines for entries and criteria for selecting winners. Publicize your contest and plan ways to use entries effectively to increase public sensibility to environmental concerns.

OR

Have a debate, discussion, or create a media event on a topic related to environmental quality, such as "Humans have the right to exploit the environment" vs. "Humans have the responsibility to preserve the environment."

11. Create and give a play, a puppet show, or a slide show to help a group in your community become more aware of the effects of pollution on the environment, wildlife, or human health. How did your audience respond to your presentation? You might follow through with a joint project that would involve them in Eco-Action, too.

*12. Make a map of your neighborhood that shows environmental quality factors, such as noise, smell, housing density, recreation facilities, and open space. Pick one problem that interests you, and find out all you can about it. List possible solutions and their implications. Use one of your solutions to design a project to improve the environmental quality of your neighborhood. You can make a difference!

Horse Sense

Horseback riding is more than caring about horses or riding "tall in the saddle." A horse is a living emotional creature, and the rider needs to understand her horse's habits, peculiarities, needs, and limitations. Whether you own your own horse, frequent a nearby stable, or take part in a riding program at camp or elsewhere, this interest project will give you a chance to increase your riding skills, gain familiarity with many aspects of horsemanship, explore the vocations and avocations dealing with riding, share your skills with others, and increase your riding confidence and pleasure.

Complete eight activities, including the five that are starred.

1. Learn what to look for in a horse and why. Consider personality traits, physical assets and defects, age, size, previous training, learning ability, response to command, appearance, and conformation. Note the strong points of conformation and why they are desirable. Find out what faults a horse might have and how they may be corrected. Using the information you have found, select a horse that would be suitable for you and your riding style (either to buy or from among the horses at the stable where you ride).

2. List ten careers related to horses and explore the four careers that interest you most. Include in your exploration the education or training required, salaries, chances for advancement, job market and stability, and other pros and cons of the position. What professional organizations do members of each field belong to? Give a presentation of your findings to a troop or group.

*3. Increase your skills in your favorite style of riding. Whether you prefer to ride English or Western, consult with a knowledgeable person. You could also consult books on the style of riding you have chosen. Find out what you have to do and then practice.

*4. Learn about tack. Keeping your style of riding and the horse or horses you ride in mind, choose several different saddles, bits, girths, and pads, and know the advantages and disadvantages of each.

Learn how to care for riding and training tack. Be able to recognize tack that has become unsafe through wear or accident. Explain and/or demonstrate the different types of tack and equipment and their care to a group of beginning riders.

*5. With permission, visit three stables and compare the differences in the following:

- boarding prices
- stall accommodations
- water drainage
- storage of hay and feed
- number of horses
- feeding schedules
- types of riding rings and trail system
- amount of pasture
- types of bedding
- method of manure disposal
- quality and amount of water readily available to horses.

Keep a record of your findings.

OR

For a minimum of three months, track the financial responsibilities involved in owning a horse. Include the initial cost of the horse (assuming you were to purchase one), the tack, farrier's bills, veterinarian's bills, training, supplies, equipment, etc. From these figures, estimate the yearly cost of ownership. You may also need to include other expenses, such as show fees, riding instruction, and transportation, if they apply. How would these considerations change if you co-owned or leased your horse?

6. Know the daily routine and equipment needed for grooming a horse. Groom a horse regularly for a period of time. Groom it as if it were going to be in a show, keeping in mind the grooming standards for this breed of horse.

*7. Know those features that distinguish the particular breed of horse that you own or would like to own. Be able to describe a horse of this breed, using proper terminology. Know what characterizes a particularly fine example of this breed.

OR

Enter a horse show, rodeo, or gymkhana. Know what the judges will be looking for in the particular event in which you will be competing.

*8. Learn how to do the following safely: groom, lead, tie, bridle, saddle, and mount a horse; hold a horse for a farrier and/or veterinarian; and catch a horse when you are on foot. Know and practice safety rules around and on horses, in the stable or ring, or on the trail. Know and practice riding courtesy.

9. Help plan and/or take part in a group overnight trail ride. Pack gear on a saddle horse and packhorse, utilize camping skills, and maintain a string of horses and their tack while on the trail.

OR

Take part in a series of at least five group trail rides of one hour's duration or more. Demonstrate your skills as a rider and your knowledge of riding safety. On one of the rides, include a cookout or a trail meal you carry with you.

10. Know the general history of the horse and its use in early times. Identify at least 10 different breeds and the specific purposes for which they are bred. Make a scrapbook of one breed, including lineage, possible registration, where the breed originated, and how it is being preserved. Give a presentation to a troop or other group on what you have learned.

11. For a series of lessons, assist a riding instructor in the teaching of riding skills. Become proficient enough to be able to teach another how to lead, saddle, bridle, groom, walk, and trot/jog a horse correctly and comfortably and how to use a crop correctly.

OR

Under the direction of a knowledgeable horse trainer, learn the following: how to longe a horse; how to teach a horse to be led; the proper use of a cavalletti; what a twitch is, and how and when it should be used.

12. Know the regular health care for a horse and the reasons for each regimen. Include worming, Coggins testing, and the vaccinations and immunizations required in your area. Know how to treat thrush, kick and puncture wounds, and general cuts, scrapes, and bites. Know when to call a veterinarian.

Know what basic items to include in a horse medical kit and how to use them. List the common medical emergencies that a horse might have, with their symptoms, causes, and the first-aid care they require.

OR

Follow a veterinarian on her or his horse calls to observe what she or he looks for when treating a horse. Interview a veterinarian about the advantages and disadvantages of her or his career.

Orienteering

Would you enjoy increasing your physical fitness while participating in a competitive sport that draws participants from countries around the globe? Or would you like to use map and compass skills to find your way while hiking, exploring the environment, horseback riding, or wilderness camping? If you are intrigued by these possibilities, *orienteering* may be the sport for you.

Orienteering is the rapidly growing activity of using a map and compass to navigate on land. Orienteers use map reading with the aid of a compass to find designated physical features in the landscape. Map reading and direction finding are important tools that will increase your self-confidence. You will have the opportunity to challenge yourself continuously as your skill at route finding increases. Skills that you learn will be useful all of your life.

You will find *Outdoor Education in Girl Scouting* and the resources listed at the end of this interest project very helpful in completing the activities.

Complete eight activities, including the three that are starred. (If an orienteering meet is not available in your area and you cannot do Activity 10, complete Activity 11.)

1. Obtain a United States Geological Survey (USGS) topographical map. Show that you can identify and explain the map symbols for water, vegetation, human-constructed, and contour features. Be able to explain what is meant by a *contour interval* and why it is important. Learn how to use the map scale and practice determining the actual distance between points on a map. Draw a sketch map of your neighborhood, community park, or Girl Scout camp. Be sure to include the scale and legend.

*2. Be able to identify each of the basic parts of a protractor compass. Learn to take a compass bearing from a map using a base plate protractor compass. Be able to demonstrate your skill at taking a bearing from a map and then walking to your destination. Learn two games that teach the skill of following a compass bearing. Teach these games to a group of Girl Scouts.

3. Obtain a United States Geological Survey (USGS) topographical map of your community. Learn how to orient the map to magnetic north. Practice the orienteering skill of "thumbing the map" by marking your place on the map with your thumb as you go for a walk around your neighborhood. Maintain contact with the map with your thumb at all times while keeping the map oriented.

4. Learn the difference between *geographic north* and *magnetic north*. Be able to explain what is meant by *declination*. Learn the declination for your area. On a United States Geological Survey (USGS) topographical map of your community, show how to adjust the map for declination by drawing a series of magnetic north lines on the map.

5. Determine your pace. Mark off a 100-foot (30 meters) pace course. Starting out on your right foot, walk from one end to the other in a normal manner. Count your paces (two steps equals one pace; count each time you put your left foot down). Repeat the pace course two more times. Add the total number of paces and find the average. To compute the average length of your pace, divide 100 feet (30 meters) by the average number of paces.

Then measure the distance between two known points on a map. Calculate the number of paces it will take you to walk that distance by dividing the map distance by the length of your pace. Walk the route you measured on the map while counting your paces. Did you reach your destination? How did your pace count compare with the distance you measured on the map?

Practice pace counting in hilly terrain or through dense woods. How does your pace for travel on flat land differ from walking in steeper or more difficult areas? Did you need more or fewer steps to cover the same distance?

Now that you have established the length of your pace, remember it and use your pace to measure distance wherever you travel.

6. Obtain an orienteering map and a United States Geological Survey (USGS) topographical map of the same area. Be able to describe the ways an orienteering map differs from a USGS topographical map. Contact an orienteering club or use written resources to find out the steps involved in producing a five-color orienteering map. Learn the meaning of the terms *base map*, *photogrammetry*, *field checking*, and *cartography*.

7. Work with a consultant from an orienteering club who is experienced in mapmaking or use written resources to learn the steps in developing an orienteering map from a United States Geological Survey (USGS) topographical map. Prepare an orienteering map of one acre or more. Field-check features accurately; include a legend, a scale, and contour intervals.

8. Work with members of an orienteering club or use written resources to learn how to organize an orienteering meet. Find out the duties of the meet director, registrar, course setter, and persons in charge of the start and the finish of the meet. Practice being a course setter. Use an orienteering map and set out 5 to 10 controls for a white (beginner) course.

*9. Learn to select the proper clothing and footwear to participate in an orienteering meet. Consider the time of year, the terrain, and the distance of the course. Know what to do if you become lost. Be able to explain the meaning and importance of a *safety bearing*. Show that you can follow a safety bearing to a road or major trail.

*10. Apply your knowledge. Take part in a local orienteering meet. Complete a white (beginner) or yellow (advanced beginner) level course. Compare your route choices with others. Discuss what you did well and what you might have done differently.

11. Set up an orienteering meet for Girl Scouts in your neighborhood. If possible, ask volunteers from an orienteering club to help you. Provide instruction for the participants in the use of a map and compass. Make an orienteering map available, recruit assistants, design a course, set the controls, and plan an awards ceremony.

12. Learn about people who use maps or orienteering skills as an important part of their jobs. Make a list of all of the careers that involve the significant use of a map and compass. Interview two people with such careers in person or by mail. Find out the educational requirements for their jobs and the employment opportunities in their fields.

Special Resources

For a list of orienteering clubs in the United States, contact:

United States Orienteering Federation
P.O. Box 1444
Forest Park, Georgia 30051

The following are some recommended books on orienteering:

British Orienteering Federation. *Course Planning.* 1972.

Gilchrist, Jim and Jack Lee. *Orienteering — Instructor's Manual.* Canada: Orienteering Ontario Publication, 1984.

Harvey, Robin. *Mapmaking for Orienteers.* British Orienteering Federation, 1985.

Kjellstrom, Bjorn. *Be Expert with Map and Compass.* LaPorte, Indiana: American Orienteering Service, 1967.

To obtain United States Geological Survey topographical maps, contact:

United States Geological Survey
Map Distribution
P.O. Box 25286
Federal Center
Denver, Colorado 80225

Or try your local camping or sporting goods store.

Outdoor Survival

Full of the fun and adventure of using advanced camping skills, this project offers ways to "stay alive" through simulated emergency/disaster situations. It could be the key to your own survival or the survival of members of your group in the future. The practice you will get in keeping control of yourself, analyzing a situation, planning a coping strategy, and making do with a minimum of equipment can be useful anywhere, whether you find yourself in a rare wilderness site or in an urban setting.

In the simulated emergency/disaster situation, the planners set the stage for the participants by learning what weather conditions are predicted, predetermining the equipment, food, and water sources available, the physical and emotional condition of the group members, any special problems to be solved, the length of the adventure, and specific rules to protect the health and safety of the participants. The participants must set priorities, solve the problems, and live out their reactions to the situation.

Complete eight activities, including the five that are starred.

1. Take a course with special emphasis on outdoor survival techniques, such as those offered by the American Red Cross, civil defense, search-and-rescue units, or some specialized ambulance corps. Learn what factors a human can control and those that she or he cannot control but must accept and cope with. Identify and put together your own personal packet of essentials to meet the needs for shelter, water, warmth, energy, and signaling.

2. Tour a hospital emergency room, an ambulance, and the facilities of a rescue unit, such as the police department, Civil Air Patrol, or the Coast Guard. Talk with staff members about their responsibilities, areas that they serve, what training is necessary, and the qualifications for joining their unit. Find out how to contact and when to use these services.

3. Know how to report an accident and how to get help when an accident happens to you or to someone with you in the out-of-doors. Contact a local search-and-rescue group (county sheriff's office, Civil Air Patrol, ski patrol, Coast Guard, or park security force), and learn from them the correct methods and symbols for signaling, the safe use of flares and other devices, and how to locate and contact help in an emergency. Post emergency telephone numbers in a conspicuous place at home and where group activities take place. Make up a trip plan form to file with responsible persons.

*4. Read accounts of survival experiences and endurance adventures. As a group, discuss feelings, such as fear, loneliness, confinement, freedom, joy, and togetherness, or talk about ways to deal with tensions created by thirst, hunger, pain, and panic in crisis situations. Discuss the importance of the determination to survive. Talk about the value of choosing and following a leader. Agree on ways to make decisions, such as when to turn back, to stay put, or to change plans.

*5. Discuss the quality of insulation and weatherproofing of different kinds of clothing. Discuss how you would improvise with available clothing and whatever's at hand to help someone survive in a hot desert, in a heavy rain, in a wind, or if the temperature falls below freezing.

*6. Talk about shelter needs for different situations and seasons. On a walk to a nearby park, a vacant area, or while camping, look for possible shelter sites or materials that could be used to protect you from cold, heat, lightning, or falling objects. If it is environmentally sound and permission is given, construct a shelter using found materials, fallen branches, or the natural features of the site, including snow. Otherwise, create an exhibit of small-scale models to show different ways to improvise shelters.

7. Become confident with a compass. Be able to use a compass to orient a map, to navigate accurately around obstacles, and backsight in order to return to your original location. Make up a compass game to test compass skills. Practice observation skills and get to know your local topography so you can use natural signs as well as a compass to find your direction. Demonstrate two methods to find direction without a compass. Lay a trail or plot a course for others to follow using these methods. Think about how conditions such as fog, a sandstorm, or a snow whiteout would complicate direction finding.

*8. Discuss the priorities of survival. List the essentials for life and write down how long the body can function without air, warmth, water, food, and rest. Brainstorm strategies and attitudes that could help you through a survival situation. Rate all the ideas and list criticisms of any plans that don't put body management first. Describe situations that show why your brain might be called "the most important thing in your survival kit."

9. Learn how to find water sources, such as by the lay of the land or vegetation patterns. Demonstrate methods of water collection and purification. Find out from experts how to identify and find edible wild plants in your area, and how such foods should be prepared or stored for use. If it is environmentally wise, and you are sure the wild plants are edible, taste and/or prepare some for your group. Learn how you could provide water and food for a group under several emergency situations. For example, if you were all snowed in or marooned, how could you make a one-day supply of water and food last for three days? Know where and how to make and use a cat hole for disposal of human waste.

10. Know when, where, and how to safely improvise fires for signaling, warming, drying, lighting, and cooking. Without using a match, show at least two ways to light a fire. Light and maintain a fire under difficult conditions, such as on a wet day or in a deep snow. Produce a fire without wood fuel. Extinguish fires safely and leave no environmental trace. Know when and where fires should not be used.

11. Using the first-aid skill and survival training you already have, plus any special training needed, volunteer your services. Work with a search-and-rescue squad, ski patrol, park security force, civil defense, or some similar group. Set up a system for calling your group together to help in an emergency.

*12. Complete all other starred requirements before undertaking this simulation activity. Reread the description of a simulation situation in the introduction to this adventure, then set the stage for a simulation activity, using one or more of the following survival situations. Then, in groups of two or four, carry out one of the simulations for at least a 12-hour period. The simulation could be:

- Your group is isolated on the edge of a cliff after a rock slide...

- Your group is adrift in a lifeboat...

- Your group's car ran out of gas while crossing the desert...

- A flash flood has swept away most of your camping gear, including your survival kit and car. The water is still cresting...

- A sudden blizzard has caught you while skiing in the mountains...

- The airplane you are on is downed in backcountry...

- You are in your city apartment when a major blackout occurs...

- Or design your own situation.

After the simulation, evaluate how well you and your group coped with stress and used your heads. Ask yourselves how well you think you'd do in a real survival situation.

Paddle, Pole, and Roll

Before beginning this interest project, you should be currently enrolled in or have completed a basic canoe or kayak course. In addition, you should have demonstrated your swimming skill and knowledge of water safety by passing the preliminary swim test as follows:

Swim Test In the presence of a lifeguard, after pitching into the water, the girl should be able to right herself and come to the surface. She should then stay afloat for five minutes by treading water, swimming with minimum progress, or resting in a floating position. This test should be conducted while the individual is clothed, including shoes.[1]

— *Lifesaving: Rescue and Water Safety,*
The American Red Cross, 1974

[1]Clothes and shoes should not be removed if you accidentally fall into the water as they can act as flotation devices and can help prevent hypothermia.

While taking part in this interest project you should, at all times, use the correct strokes as outlined in the American Red Cross manual, *Canoeing and Kayaking,* and observe the standards in *Safety-Wise.* You will need to wear a personal flotation device (PFD) when participating in any small craft activity.

Complete eight activities, including the two that are starred.

*1. Show your consultant/instructor that you can handle your craft (canoe or kayak) by demonstrating the following:

 • Keep your craft going in a straight line to a designated point for a distance of 50 yards (approximately 46 meters).

 • Keep your craft going backward in a straight line to a designated point for a distance of 50 yards (approximately 46 meters).

 • Propel your craft sideways for five yards (approximately 4.6 meters).

 • Make your craft do a right turn, a left turn, and a 360° turn.

 • Trim (balance) your craft while boarding and launching it. Demonstrate the three-point contact for rough and windy weather.

 • Demonstrate your ability to start, stop, dock, and beach your craft.

2. To keep your equipment in good working order, show that you know the procedures for maintenance and care of your craft. Demonstrate your knowledge of the procedures for storage and transport of your craft. Also, know how to make the necessary emergency repairs while on a run, such as what to do if the craft:

 • springs a leak or becomes punctured

 • breaks ribs or thigh braces

 • bends gunwales.

3. Know and be able to identify the major parts of a canoe and/or kayak and the major differences in materials used in making them. Draw a diagram of the craft and label the parts. In addition, know and be able to identify the types of paddles and poles and the materials used to make them. Demonstrate your knowledge of the paddle by explaining to a group the different types of paddles, the advantage of using each, and why you chose your paddle.

4. Demonstrate that you know the proper attire for canoeing and/or kayaking in all types of weather. Show how to choose a PFD of proper size and adjust it to fit. Be sure to include a discussion on hypothermia. For example, set up a display on proper attire for your troop meeting, camping trip, community event, or local mall display area, or have a fashion show for a younger troop.

5. After consultation with your instructor/consultant, simulate four of the following six situations and demonstrate to your troop or group how you would handle them. (Remember to use *Safety-Wise* as a reference.) You should know how to handle all six of these situations:

   • A medical emergency arises, such as cold or heat stress.

   • A person is thrown into fast-moving water with one person still in the craft.

   • A craft is overturned. Two victims are in the water, one with a broken arm, one with no PFD.

   • A paddle catches on a tree limb and is lost.

   • A craft is overturned, with two victims in water, both suffering from hypothermia.

   • There is lightning, or severe storm conditions exist.

*6. Help plan and take part in at least a two-day canoe/kayak trip. Learn to read the water conditions and know the international scale of difficulty. Demonstrate awareness of skills, strategies, and knowledge necessary for a safe trip. If possible, include a portage on your trip and demonstrate the skills necessary to complete it safely and skillfully.

7. Learn to make or teach someone else to make an article of equipment — for example, a thigh strap, pole, bailer, paddle, throw rope bag, or knee pads — that you could use while canoeing or kayaking.

OR

Chart on a map, or make a listing of, the canoe/kayak trails within a hundred miles of your Girl Scout meeting place and the liveries and/or canoe campsites and takeout sites located near them. Share copies with your council, chamber of commerce, and GSUSA.

OR

Help develop a detailed canoe/kayak trail guide of a single navigable river or waterway. Include some interesting facts about the area, such as its geology, animal and plant life, and ecology.

8. Put on a canoe/kayak skill and safety demonstration in a swimming pool for other Girl Scouts.

9. Do two of three:

   • Advance your swimming skills by taking a course in survival swimming, emergency water safety, or lifeguarding.

   • Take a course in map and compass use and/or orienteering.

   • Take a course in outdoor survival.

10. Choose one of the following groups — voyageurs (fur traders and explorers), American Indians, or Pacific Islanders — and trace the role of their craft in the development of this country. Make a poster, display, or scrapbook of what you found out and share it with another group.

11. Find out about the canoe/kayak events that are part of the national, international, or Olympic scene. Contact one of the canoe associations to see if there are any national or international competitions scheduled for television and, if there are, watch them to see the different types of courses and events that are included. Share your findings with your troop or group.

OR

Take part in a local canoe competition or regatta by helping set up the course or becoming a participant in the event.

12. The lure of the water calls to many. Discover the excitement for yourself. Learn about the lore, legend, and songs of the water. Take part in a sunrise watch and then share observations with others by trying your hand at a poem, song, or short story.

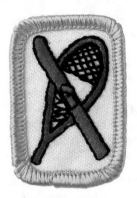

Skiing and Snowshoeing

Cold weather offers wonderful opportunities for outdoor activities. When you are well prepared, the crisp, cold air can be refreshing and invigorating. In this interest project you can improve your skills in cross-country skiing, downhill skiing, or snowshoeing. Each of these activities can lead to exciting new places, breathtaking vistas, and an appreciation of the creatures that survive in subfreezing temperatures.

It is important that you be prepared for cold-weather adventures — physically fit, well nourished, and adequately clothed to withstand the conditions. Equally important is having equipment that is safe and properly fitted to you. Take lessons in your chosen sport to learn the proper techniques and safety rules. Take time to enjoy the beauty of a landscape of snow and ice, too!

Complete A, B, or C and six additional requirements, including those that are starred. If your skills are beyond the level described in A, B, or C for your chosen sport when you start this project, or if you have a disability, work with a qualified instructor to establish a set of goals for you to accomplish within a season. Use those goals to measure your skills for this requirement.

A. *CROSS-COUNTRY SKIING — EQUIPMENT*
Be able to describe the differences between kinds of cross-country skis, boots, and bindings. Compare waxable and waxless skis. Show that you know how to measure skis and poles for your height and weight. Which skis would you choose to purchase and why? Demonstrate how you would carry, maintain, and store your skis.

CROSS-COUNTRY SKIING — TECHNIQUE
Show that you have mastered the techniques of kick and glide, double poling, skiing up steep hills using side stepping and the herringbone step, skiing downhill, the pole drag, the kick turn, the step turn, and snowplow stops and turns. Demonstrate how to stand up after a fall. Show how to grip the poles properly. Know when *not* to use the pole straps.

B. *DOWNHILL SKIING — EQUIPMENT*
Describe how to insert and release a ski boot from a ski binding. Tell how the binding holds the boot to the ski. Find out from someone who services bindings how the DIN setting is determined. Show how to carry, care for, maintain, and store your ski equipment properly. Explain the function of ski brakes and powder straps. Explain why one might choose short or long skis.

DOWNHILL SKIING — TECHNIQUE
Show your skills on the slopes by demonstrating that you can comfortably do the following: snowplow turns, snowplow stop, linked christie turns (stem or parallel) with a traverse between the turns, parallel stop, sideslipping, side stepping, and herringbone. Show the proper use of the poles while doing each of these skills. Show that you know how to use two different kinds of lifts. Learn and then tell the meaning of the standard signs that indicate trail difficulty. Discuss the rules of safety and etiquette on the slopes and in lift lines.

C. *SNOWSHOEING — EQUIPMENT*
Explain how snowshoes enable you to walk across the surface of the snow. Be able to describe the differences in the design between bearpaw, Green Mountain bearpaw, Michigan, and Alaskan snowshoes. What are the advantages of each style of snowshoe? Which one would you choose and why? Describe the different snowshoe bindings. Under what conditions would you use each one? Explain the care and maintenance required for wooden frame snowshoes and rawhide or neoprene webbings.

SNOWSHOEING — TECHNIQUE

Demonstrate that you can walk comfortably in snowshoes. Show that you can do a step turn and kick turn, walk uphill and downhill, and use crampons. Explain the method for breaking a trail. Be able to discuss the hazards of snowshoeing in potential avalanche areas and crossing snow-covered lakes.

*1. Show how you would dress for the sport you have chosen. Be able to explain the advantages of dressing in layers. Cold-weather clothing is made of a wide variety of materials. Compare the different fabrics and types of insulation. Be able to explain what clothing you would select to conserve your body heat, to allow perspiration to escape, and to keep out wind and water. Show the types of eye protection worn for these sports.

*2. Under the guidance of a physical fitness professional, create an exercise program designed to increase your muscular strength, endurance, and flexibility. Develop a cardiovascular fitness plan. Follow the exercise and cardiovascular fitness plan for two months and keep a chart to monitor your progress.

3. Complete a first-aid course. Assemble a portable first-aid kit for your sports activities. Be able to control bleeding, administer artificial respiration, treat for shock, treat fractures, sprains, strains, frostbite, sunburn, and snow blindness. Explain what is meant by *hypothermia* and how to treat and prevent it. Know how to report an accident and how to summon help.

4. Check the weather forecast before you spend a day outdoors. Be able to explain the importance of a rising or falling barometer, a warm or cold front, and the windchill factor. Learn to interpret the cloud and wind signs in your area that indicate changing weather conditions. Learn how snow and ice conditions change in different weather conditions.

5. Plan a snowshoeing or skiing outing for other girls in your neighborhood. Select a site, arrange the transportation, and see that equipment and instruction are available.

6. Interview a person whose job includes winter sports and find out how she or he became involved. Examples include a ski patrol member, a ski instructor, a ski-equipment salesperson, or an operator of a ski area.

7. Share the beauty of the winter environment with others by writing poetry or prose about it, taking photographs and showing them to others, or creating an expressive dance or skit.

8. Learn about the qualities of snow. For example, what happens during freezing and sublimation? What are the effects of snow and cold temperatures on plants and animals? Catch snowflakes and observe their shapes and sizes.

9. Learn how mammals cope with cold weather. Find out about one mammal that hibernates during the winter. If possible, observe one mammal that is active during such periods. How does it move about? How does it find its food? Record the pattern and size of its tracks in the snow.

OR

Maintain a bird-feeding station through the winter months. Keep a record of the species and numbers of birds that use it. Record how their behavior changes when the weather changes. Observe bird life while participating in a winter sport and compare your findings with those from the feeding station.

Smooth Sailing

Sailing in harmony with the water and the wind, you'll feel an exhilarating "lift" from being airborne through the water. To be a safe skipper or crew member, you must feel confident *in* the water and pass the following swim test before going *on* the water:

In the presence of a lifesaver, after pitching into the water, the girl should be able to right herself and come to the surface. She should then stay afloat for five minutes by treading water, swimming with minimum progress, or resting in a floating position. This test should be conducted while the individual is clothed, including shoes.

— *Lifesaving: Rescue and Water Safety,*
American Red Cross, 1974

For any activities on or near the water, you should be accompanied by a qualified adult. Smart sailors will take a course to help them progress through the Smooth Sailing interest project. You may be staying close to shore or venturing on blue waters, sailing a dinghy, a sailboard, a sloop, or a schooner. Remember, your best is the least that's expected.

Complete eight activities, including the four that are starred. These are for safety. Complete them before getting underway under sail.

*1. Prepare to be safe and feel good. Learn how to do everything on the following checklist. Then refer to the checklist every time you sail to be sure you have made these essential preparations.

  • Wear and care for a personal flotation device (PFD) that is Coast Guard approved. Be sure it is the right type, size, and fit, and that you can put it on while treading water. Review the H.E.L.P. (heat-escape-lessening-positions) and huddle to prevent hypothermia. Remember that you must wear your PFD at all times while on the small craft.

  • Choose and wear the right footwear, hat, and clothing to prevent harmful exposure to the elements, whether it's cold, hot, sunny, or rainy.

  • Choose and use the proper sunglasses, sunscreen, and lip balm to protect your eyes and skin.

  • Be up-to-date on first aid for near-drowning, hypothermia, and heatstroke.

  • Pack, stow, and secure whatever water and food you'll need. Be prepared to dispose of waste properly.

  • Do a safety check to show that all required and desired gear is working and stowed properly (extra line; bailer, pump, or sponge; paddle; etc.).

  • File a float plan. Be sure someone responsible ashore knows where you'll be sailing, who's going with you, and when you expect to return. Let her or him know when you're back safely or if your plan changes.

*2. Learn to watch the wind, water, and weather patterns for your sailing area. Make a list of safe-weather rules to match the boat and your abilities. Considering wave heights and wind speed, set limits on when not to go out, when to run for the closest shelter, and when to head for home. Always think of thunderstorms as an emergency.

  • Get the general forecast from the newspaper, television, or radio. Predict local conditions, using a barometer, storm signals, and/or NOAA radio or telephone.

  • Figure the time of sunrise, sunset, currents, and/or tides if they'll affect your sailing.

  • Tell wind direction and estimate wind speed from telltales, flags, the wind's effect on the boat, and wave heights and other water conditions.

- Monitor weather conditions by clouds and wind shifts. When underway, constantly check weather changes against the limits you've set for being on the water.

*3. Go by the Coast Guard motto, "Semper Paratus," and be "always ready" to help a boater in distress, including yourself. Learn to manage risky sailing situations with an a-b-c approach:

   a. *Practical prevention.* Pay attention to details for signs of danger. Keep your skills sharp, and your safety gear and your boat shipshape.

   b. *Right reaction.* Practice the best first response until it becomes an automatic habit.

   c. *Sensible solution.* Quickly think through all you *could* do. Carefully decide what you *should* do to resolve the situation.

   Make a card for each of the following situations and add any more that might threaten you. Then write, memorize, and practice (a) Prevention, (b) Reaction, and (c) Solution for each situation.

   - falling overboard
   - capsizing
   - leaking, swamping, sinking
   - lines, sails, rig, or steering gear out of control (failed, fouled, or whipping free)
   - contact with overhead power lines or electrical cords in the water
   - high winds
   - rough waters
   - fog, dark (reduced visibility)
   - fire
   - going aground
   - local situations.

*4. Make a checklist for getting ready to sail and keeping shipshape. Call things by their nautical names as you show how to do at least three of the following;

   - Rig, handle, derig, and store the parts, rig and rigging, fittings, lines, and sails.
   - Tie and use the bowline, figure eight (stopper), and reef knot. Use the proper hitches to tie to a post, a ring, and a cleat. Handle line — show how to get kinks out, make up a coil, and get line clear to run. Show you can hoist or haul away, lower or ease, tail, hold, take a turn, take up slack, and make fast. Practice throwing a line — for docking, towing, or with a life ring to a target in the water.

- Roll, fold, bag, and/or stow sails.
- Maintain or make something useful. Whip or splice a line, patch or mend a sail, renew a block, refasten a fitting, make a heaving line or a ditty bag.

5. Concentrate on launching, leaving, and landing. Show how to do the following:

   - Launch and/or load the boat. Board and load the boat to keep it in trim. Show how and where to step aboard, to sit, and to move around in the boat. Go over your safety checklist before getting underway.
   - Get underway from a ramp, mooring, dock, or anchorage.
   - Pick up a mooring, come alongside, make a landing, or anchor. Place and secure fenders, chafing gear, and lines as needed.

6. Master maneuvering. First, learn and show off the safety position. (Stop by letting the sails out and luff with the wind about on the beam.) Then demonstrate how to do the following:

   - Stop, start, and "get out of irons."
   - Head up, bear away, and reduce excessive heel.
   - Steer with the sails.
   - Go forward, backward, and sideways (make headway, sternway, and leeway).
   - Tack and jibe (gybe) safely. (Get used to the right terms and responses: "Ready about!" "Ready." "Hard alee," etc.)
   - Do a "man overboard" drill and/or pick up a towline.

7. Sail an upwind, downwind, and crosswind course. Show the effect of lift and luff, angle of attack, and true and apparent wind. Explain how a sail and a wing work alike. Sail a circular course and point out the points of sail. Steer by a range of landmarks or a compass. Make good a course and round a mark.

8. Avoid collisions!

   - Find out about the rules of the road. Describe when to keep the right-of-way (stand on) and when to yield (give way): for example, when a sailboat meets, crosses, or overtakes another sailboat, powerboat, and canoe or rowboat.
   - Learn how to keep a good lookout and report relative bearings of things around your imaginary bow, beam, and stern. Tell how to know if you're on a collision course. Figure and describe alternative ways to avoid collisions for different points of sail.

9. Know how to get where you want to go. Be able to tell direction by the sun and the stars. Then do *one* of the following:

   • Make or read a chart of the waters you sail. Using symbols, locate landmarks, ranges, and aids to navigation. Also locate hazards such as overhead power lines; rocks, shoals, and shallows; swimming, diving, or waterskiing areas. Note launch ramps and places where the public has access to the water.

   OR

   Plot the courses for a day's run. Figure the true, magnetic, and compass courses. Practice dead reckoning, taking bearings, fixing position, and estimating time of arrival. Make notes on highlights and hazards along the way. Figure the latitude and longitude of your home port.

10. Highlight good sportsmanship as you do two of the following activities related to racing under sail:

    Fine tune for speed. As crew or skipper, show how to get the most out of the boat, figuring when and how much to adjust your weight, sails, lines, centerboard, and rig for a "perfect" start, rounding a mark, and tacking.

    OR

    Learn the special rules that ensure "fair play" in racing. Show good sportsmanship in a race or serve on a race committee.

    OR

    Research at least two famous record holders — *Cutty Sark, Bluenose*, schooner *America, Australia II*, and *Stars and Stripes*, for example — and describe what made them winners.

11. Report on interviews or readings about at least two people for whom sailing is a way to make a living and/or a way of life. These people can be involved in sailing for recreation or pay, for example: someone who cruises, crews, or skippers; a sailing instructor; a marina operator; a boat builder; a sail maker; a yacht broker; a deckhand; a ship's cook; a licensed captain; or a worker in a related career.

12. Bring some maritime heritage to life. Learn and teach an "old salt's" skill such as scrimshaw, fancy knots (macramé), ship modeling, or chantey singing.

    OR

    Read a ship's log or visit a maritime museum or a historic sailing ship like *Elissa, Star of India, Peking, USS Constitution, C. A. Thayer*, or *Ernestina*.

    OR

    Make a presentation about "Tall Ships" or go aboard a sail-training ship like USCG *Eagle, Joseph Conrad*, or *Adventuress*.

Water Sports

For many people, the roar of surf, the deep end of a pool, the diving platform, the helm, and the paddle are irresistible. In fact, anything to do with water is fine with them. Perhaps you feel the same way, but think you have to be a superswimmer to enjoy water sports. Not so. However, you will need to wear a personal flotation device (PFD) when participating in any of these small craft activities. Also, while some "dry-land" activities can be done alone, taking a buddy on the water and having a lifeguard available are musts.

If you choose this project, you must first pass the preliminary swim test. The test is as follows:

In the presence of a lifeguard, after pitching into the water, the girl should be able to right herself and come to the surface. She should then stay afloat for five minutes by treading water, swimming with minimum progress, or resting in a floating position. This test should be conducted while the individual is clothed, including shoes.

— *Lifesaving: Rescue and Water Safety,*
American Red Cross, 1974

You'll find that, even if you have limited access to a pool or waterfront, you will still have enough choices to finish this project.

If your aim is to qualify for a waterfront job at a Girl Scout camp, see *Girl Scout Camping Guidelines* and choose activities accordingly.

Complete eight activities, including the one that is starred.

*1. Demonstrate basic self-rescue in the water, with and without a PFD. Complete a swimming, emergency water safety, lifeguarding, or boating-safety course to advance your skills in water safety.

2. Learn and practice ways to prevent harmful effects of sun, wind, and water. Demonstrate your ability to recognize and treat sunburn, heatstroke, heat cramps, heat exhaustion, hypothermia, frostbite, and seasickness. Show how to revive a person who has stopped breathing.

3. Demonstrate at least three basic strokes, showing coordination and versatility. Measure your endurance and set a goal to improve it. Participate in one of the following: competitive, synchronized, or therapeutic swimming or aid in giving swimming lessons.

4. Before rowing, canoeing, sailing, rafting, or motoring, first equip the watercraft for safety. Demonstrate the proper use of each piece of equipment. Show that you know what to do if a boat swamps or overturns, and if someone falls overboard. With any small craft, demonstrate that you can handle it safely, including how to launch, board and debark, load and trim, get underway, maneuver, and either anchor, moor, beach, dock, or trailer it.

5. Describe the hazards of diving and ways to prevent diving accidents, such as checking for obstructions in the diving area, holding hands firmly overhead in all headfirst dives, not running on deck or the diving board, etc. Describe the basic parts of a dive, the positions, and the diving groups. Demonstrate two dives from a springboard, showing your coordination.

6. Learn how to snorkel under qualified instruction. Show proper fit and use of mask, snorkel, and fins. Demonstrate moving on the surface, submerging, underwater movement, and rescue skills. Practice ways to leave underwater life and habitats undisturbed.

7. With an experienced water-ski instructor or advanced skier, learn and observe the Water Skiers' Safety Code (American Water Ski Association). Demonstrate the proper use of signals for the boat driver, the safety observer, and the skier. Adjust PFD and ski bindings to fit and demonstrate the proper position for a deep-

water start. Show that you can "get up," control your balance, maneuver, land, fall, and recover your skis safely.

OR

If you are an accomplished ocean swimmer, learn to ride the waves with an experienced instructor or advanced surfer. Discuss your knowledge of ocean conditions, such as the bottom, tides, currents, and wave action. In surf that matches your ability, demonstrate ways to avoid falling off your board, and ways of falling or diving from the board safely. Discuss and demonstrate ways of controlling the board.

8. Learn the rules and take part in or observe a water sport, like water polo, a swim or diving meet, a canoe slalom, a sailing race, or a fishing derby. Find out about the early development of a water sport, when it became popular, what records have been set, and who some of its stars have been. Make up a water game, adapting a land favorite to a water setting. Share some of your enthusiasm with a landlubber, helping her or him feel knowledgeable as an observer or comfortable as a participant in a water sport or game.

9. On a map or nautical chart, locate places where the public has access to water for recreation. Identify residential, commercial, disposal, transportation, and/or historic waterfront areas. Attend a hearing or do a project concerned with cooperative use or preservation of waterfront property.

OR

Identify some countries or areas where water skills are an important part of the way of life. Find out how the skills are passed on and what kind of conditioning is necessary. Describe symbols, relate legends, or share songs that reflect the culture's emphasis on water.

10. Monitor the water quality at a recreation area, such as a pool, lake, beach, or farm pond. Either test the quality of water at the same location at several different times or compare water quality from several sources. (Applies to qualifications for Girl Scout camp aquatics/waterfront assistant.)

OR

For a waterfront area you know, find out about hazardous current, wave, or tidal conditions, obstructions or bottom hazards, and dangerous water life. Set up a system to warn others of such hazards. (Applies to qualifications for Girl Scout camp lifesaver/guard.)

11. Help make, maintain, or preserve a piece of equipment, a boat, or other structure that has to withstand a watery environment.

OR

Create something using fancy knots or natural materials found on or near the shore.

12. Take a trip by water (See Travel, pages 59–60). Learn and follow the nautical rules-of-the-road for waters you'll be traveling.

OR

Get involved in a swim show, regatta, harbor day, water festival, sail-training event, mariner gam (gathering of sea people), or other water-oriented special activity.

Wildlife

Have you ever watched a hawk soar over a meadow? met a fox while hiking a trail? seen a school of fish surface? watched a sparrow choose a nesting place in the city? If you have, you probably can recall the wonder and joy of each particular moment. But how long will such experiences be available to the inhabitants of planet Earth?

As communities grow and encroach on areas formerly uninhabited by humans, habitats crucial to wildlife are being reduced or eradicated. The critical balances of the ecosystem are being changed, perhaps forever, by interference in wildlife needs for available food, water, and space for living and raising young.

With those who do scientific studies, as well as those who enjoy recreation in the out-of-doors, you'll grow to realize how increasing rates of change around us are affecting wildlife, too.

Like millions of people, you too can enjoy studying wildlife with binoculars, camera, tape recorder, sketch pad, or notebook in hand — or simply feel the peace that comes from being in the wild. And through this interest project, you can consider reasonable choices and act on well-informed decisions for the future of wildlife in this country and in your own community.

Complete eight activities, including the one that is starred.

1. Find a natural area or vacant lot that you can study. Make at least four trips to the site and do the following:

   • Describe the kinds of rocks found in the area.

   • Dig a soil sample, measure the layers, and record their characteristics.

   • Make notes recording the temperature, wind direction, weather conditions, date, and time of day.

   • Record the names of plants found in the area.

   • Record the names of animals seen in the area.

   • After your fourth visit, describe what influence soil and weather have on the plants and animals.

2. Show that you know the meaning of the following words by making up a game that will help someone else learn them: *predator, prey, herbivore, carnivore, omnivore, decomposer, wildlife community, food web.*

3. Watch a group of the same kind of animal, such as ants, pigeons, rabbits, or fish. How are individuals similar in their behavior? different in their behavior? When, how, and what do they eat? Describe interactions between individuals. Figure out the amount of space each individual needs. Record your observations.

   OR

   Watch one animal closely. Record behavior patterns related to eating, to protection, to providing for other needs, and to defending a territory. Note and record which ones are repeated frequently. Also record behaviors that show an animal using its senses and responding to its environment.

   OR

   Without injuring the plant, design an experiment to show how a plant reacts to its environment. Record or illustrate what happens.

4. Find out how insecticides and herbicides travel through the ecosystem. Describe the process of biological magnification and its effects on predators.

5. Visit a wildlife refuge, wildlife management area, nature center, or natural park to learn how it is managed for wildlife. Find out the difference between a management area and a wilderness. Plan and carry out a project that will benefit wildlife.

   OR

   Find out about the career opportunities available in working with wildlife.

6. Find out the meaning of the terms *threatened, endangered,* and *extinct* wildlife. Choose one endangered species native to the United States. Find out why it has become endangered and what is being done to help it survive. Decide what you can do to help and then do it.

*7. Choose a category of wildlife for in-depth study — birds, mammals, insects, reptiles, amphibians, fish, trees, herbaceous plants. Then, learn to identify 15 species in their natural settings and be able to identify them in all seasons and/or stages.

Choose 5 of the 15 and learn for each:

• its habitat requirements

• what affects the numbers in its population

• its life history

• how it fits into a food chain.

With this information, give reasons why habitat preservation is a key to wildlife survival.

8. Locate organizations in your area interested in wildlife preservation. Attend one of their meetings or field trips. Ask for help in learning how or where you can observe wildlife, or participate in one of their projects.

9. With the cooperation of your Girl Scout council, make a survey of one campsite. Inventory the property to list the kinds of plants and animals found there. With some expert help, plan and carry out a project to benefit the wildlife or a project to share your wildlife knowledge with others, such as through a Lou Henry Hoover Memorial Sanctuary.

10. Design a project that will improve a wildlife habitat in your neighborhood. Carry out the project and record the results.

11. When plants and animals from other countries are released in the United States, many die for lack of the proper environment; others have successfully competed with native wildlife. Discover how and why one of the following has been successful: nutria, walking catfish, English sparrow, starling, pheasant, fire ant, gypsy moth, eucalyptus, water hyacinth, dandelion, or other animal or plant common to your area.

12. Find out about the international laws that affect the protection and trade of wildlife products. Find out what is happening to wildlife in developing countries around the world.

OR

Find out about the federal and state laws that protect wildlife in the United States. Copies of bills and laws can be obtained through the office of an elected representative in your political district. Write a bill for the protection of wildlife that you would like to see enacted. Role-play with a group the path your bill would follow on its way through the legislative process.

Index